Unseen H

A Journey of Faith, Family and Second Chances

5-1-2020

Karen Ryan –

Sorry this took so long to get to you. You and your family will always be family to us. We are eternally grateful for your love, care, generosity and grace you've showered on us through the years. God bless you, your family, and all those you touch.

Rich Lupia

Rich Lupia
Edited by Kevin DeValk

Share Your Story and Give God the Glory

ISBN: 9781726814201
© 2020 Lupia & Associates LLC
All rights reserved.
No part of this book may be used in any way without giving credit to the author, in person or in any form of traditional or digital media including social media.

Scripture quotations are from the ESV® Bible (The Holy Bible, English Standard Version®), copyright © 2001 by Crossway, a publishing ministry of Good News Publishers. Used by permission. All rights reserved.

Table of Contents

Introduction	**1**
1) Near suicide	7
2) Heart Level	13
3) Saved!	17
4) How did I stop?	20
5) The struggles	23
6) Mission accomplished	25
7) The waiting and more struggling	29
8) El Capitan and Half Dome	32
9) Meeting Amy	34
10) The choice	37
11) The dream comes true	39
12) Never the same	44
13) Hail of change	47
14) What's happening to Amy?	52
15) Cancer and the prediction	55
16) Please don't let Zack die	57
17) 40 days and 40 nights Part 1	59
18) The prayer for more children	64
19) Emergency respite	67
20) Can't utter the word "no"	70
21) Adoption	75
22) Mount Marcy	79
23) Celebration!	84
24) Goodbye Tom	86
25) Brain tumor	90
26) 40 days and 40 nights Part 2	93
27) Goodbye Mamwah	96
28) Weak and weary	99
29) Acceptance	103
30) Floodgates	105
31) Looking to the future	111
32) Second Chances	115
About the author	120
Acknowledgements	121

*For my God, my wife, my family,
my friends and all who are holding this book:*

I'm so blessed by you. Thank you.

Introduction

You can't have a testimony without a "test".

We like to avoid them, but they usually find us, the tests of life. Sometimes we bring them on ourselves. This book could be 500 chapters, but 32 is plenty. Why did I write this? We are so good at putting up a façade, with a smiling face, saying everything is great! We all do this, but behind the façade, many of us are hurting. We feel all alone in our suffering. We think no one else could understand the troubles we go through. We want to cry out for help, but the fear of being rejected furthers our pain.

We are experts at making our lives look, literally, "picture perfect" on Facebook and Instagram. We look strong and confident on Twitter and LinkedIn. We play the game at work, with friends and family, and in church. It's time to be honest with ourselves and each other. We all have our own mountains to climb and we wonder if we'll ever get there at all. Clearly there is one thing that has died out of us as a people, besides common courtesy, respect and kindness to each other…

Hope.

I'm no pastor. I'm no theologian. But I am a believer in God, in his son Jesus Christ and I do have a testimony. I have my story of what God has done in my life and is continuing to do that is unmistakable. Despite what could have been certain death or disaster for me and my family, God has brought me through the fire and is continuing to refine me.

I was born in Utica, NY, upstate New York, which is much more like the middle American rust belt than the cosmopolitan New York City. I was born into a large Catholic family, Italian on my dad's side, German on my mom's. My story starts with incredible pain and struggle through my teen years and high school which nearly broke me, out the other side to college to realize my lifelong dream, to finding an incredible woman to share the rest of my life, with the ups and downs of marriage and raising children. All of this while trying to keep from going off the rails.

I still have a long way to go. We all do! Here's the thing: You probably have stories and testimonies that will make my story pale in comparison. These are the stories that could change lives for the better, even for those you care about around you. So why haven't you shared them? Because we are scared to now. Look around at how people have become.

As a Gen-X'er, I've seen the culture go from old school respect for elders, those in authority, and God to a narcissistic culture, atheistic (or at least agnostic) and more hostile to traditional family and Christian values. We used to look out for each other. We used to think the best of each other. The hope we had as a society, and as Christians, is not there like it was. We are so scared to share our story because there could be a cost: Losing friends, relationships with family, maybe even our jobs. It's real. We've seen it happen through recent years because of social media. And so, we fake it, or we hide it to avoid the pain. I do, too. It's human.

"Beloved, do not be surprised at the fiery trial when it comes upon you to test you as though something strange were happening to you. But rejoice insofar as you share Christ's sufferings, that you may also rejoice and be glad when his glory is revealed. <u>If you are insulted for the name of Christ, you are BLESSED because the spirit of glory and of God rests upon you.</u>" 1 Peter 4:12-14 ESV

In the end, are we living for others, or what we truly believe in? Honest question. Too often, if you are honest, you'll find you are living not what you want but what others want for you. It could be for a spouse, a parent, a boss, friends or even strangers. I did just that for way too long. Is trading our best to appease others worth it? Yes, we must be mindful of those around us, especially family and those closest to us, and we need to be respectful. That doesn't mean we compromise or squelch who we truly are.

Here's the guide: *"First of all, then, I urge that supplications, prayers, intercessions, and thanksgivings be made for all people, for kings and all who are in high positions, <u>that we may lead a peaceful and quiet life, godly and dignified in every way. This is good, and it is pleasing in the sight of God our Savior, who desires all people to be saved and to come to the knowledge of the truth.</u> For there is one God, and there is one mediator between God and men, the man Christ Jesus, who gave himself as a ransom for all, <u>which is the testimony given at the proper time."</u> 1 Timothy 2:1-6 ESV*

Peaceful and quiet does not mean silent and hidden.

Testimonies give people hope that compliments, but doesn't supersede, the promises that God the father and Jesus Christ his son have left us in the Bible. Without the stories of what God is doing today, the words in the Bible, the very Gospel itself, may seem distant and irrelevant. Let me assure you the "Unseen Hand of God" is moving today. We aren't going to draw people back to God by a moral argument, judging and bashing people. All you need to do is visit your social media page as evidence that is not working at all.

To have a good testimony we need to be real.

We need to be honest with each other about how messed up and broken we are as people. We need to confess that Jesus Christ is the one to heal us from our sins and give us the gift of eternal life. The final and most important piece of the puzzle is let them see the change in our lives. In America, we are experts at," Do as I say, not as I do," or, "Say one thing and do another". We have thankfully entered a time where people are sick of the fake stuff and junk. We want everything to be real from our food, to our news, what we buy, what we see and what we do. I believe God is real, His promises are real, His son Jesus is real, He is alive today, and He can change your world in ways beyond what you can imagine.

But we struggle. We haven't figured it out. We doubt. We go along great and then we blow it bad. We embarrass ourselves. We feel bad because we've blown it, we have no credibility to speak and must stay silent. Join the club! I know this much: Past failures don't guarantee future failures, if you learn from them. We need to live with enthusiasm and passion for the God who loved you so much, He sent His son Jesus to die on a rugged cross for you. The passion and honesty for God attracts people. It also attracts detractors. Ignore the detractors and focus on what is real!

I want to be an encourager. I'm sick of seeing people hurting. I want to help as many people as I can, not for my own glory, but in thankfulness to God who gave me life more abundant in His son Jesus. As I've shared my story in person, and our family has shared our story to others, people are amazed. It has had a great and positive impact on them. I believe God has revealed this to me as an encouragement to do more. I want people to have the hope I have. I want them to know God is real and alive today, not just pages in a book. I want people to know that hope is still out there. People that care are still out there. It's not my line but it's every bit true: People don't care how much you know until they know how much you care.

We need to listen more, care more and talk less. When we do talk, be effective and intentional with a heart for truly helping others. This is a love letter to those who believe in God and in the saving power of Jesus Christ. This is also a lifeline to those in a deep and dark place as you read this. Jesus is not about a "religion", a denomination or a movement born of man. It's about God's one and only son, reaching down out of heaven to intercede for us and help those who put their trust in Him.

What if you've "tried God" or accepted Jesus as your savior in the past and have been let down terribly by other Christians? There are a lot of you out there. Chances are if you aren't one of them, you know someone who has been "religious" or claimed to be a Christian who has let you down. I know at times; I was one of them. It's so easy for people to point to us at times, say "hypocrite!" and they would be correct. Notice I said, "at times". We are human. We constantly struggle with sin and selfishness as Christians. It's those who understand that they are nothing without Jesus and humble themselves about who they are, that God uses to make our imperfections, our brokenness, perfect in Christ.

Don't give up. Keep seeking. Keep knocking. Scripture encourages that. If you keep hitting the "holier than thou" crowd, keep moving on! There are people and churches out there who want to love others, serve others, and truly help others. I wish there were more. Maybe this will be a wake-up call for some of them to get right with God and each other.

I made some big mistakes and have lived a far from perfect life, before becoming a Christian at 17 and certainly since. All the blessings I've received from being able to live out a dream career for 9 years, have a loving wife of 18 years, a great son with a big heart, three adopted children, a great extended family, great friends and a great church to belong to: **It's all despite me.**

So often I've blown it with my big mouth, or attitude, or misreading situations and opportunities. It's truly the grace of

God that I have been able to do anything good. You'll see this through the individual testimonies in this book. It's only through continued faith and trust in God to do what he has called me to do, that I'll be able to best serve. I want to serve my God, my family, my employer, my church and all others. The main objective is to give glory to God in all that I do and say. That should be the main objective for us all. Because we aren't our own, we were bought by the blood of Jesus Christ.

The Great Commission is there for a reason in Matthew 28. We're all equipped differently and will serve differently, as highlighted in 1 Corinthians 12, but not serving is not an option. Nowhere does it say in the Bible "only if you want to or if you feel like it or if it's convenient". Last time I read Matthew 5:14-16 ESV, I read this: *"You are the light of the world. A city on a hill cannot be hidden, nor do people light a lamp and put it under a basket, but on a stand, and it gives light to all in the house. In the same way, let your light shine before others, so that they may see your good works and give glory to your Father, who is in heaven."*

In short, share your story and give God the Glory.

Chapter 1
Near suicide

I was that kid.

I was the unpopular one growing up, the one everyone knew, but few knew well. I knew I wanted to be a meteorologist from a very young age. I wanted friends and wanted to have fun, but I wasn't cool enough for most kids. I had glasses by the time I was 14. Even well before that, I was a geek. I was smart, and often the outcast. I was different, and into different things than other kids.

I was bullied incessantly through elementary school and right on into secondary school. I got into so many fights where I got punched, kicked, spit on, got insults hurled at me, I lost count a long time ago. And while we grow and mature, those scars never fully healed. Even long past it at 44 years old now, it's something that subconsciously impacts you. You must remind yourself that what happened was not all your fault. You have to remind yourself of the truth.

Junior high and high school can be among the meanest and most unforgiving places on Earth. It certainly was when I was in school. Your body reaches adult height, but inside you are still a kid, trying to figure out life and your place in it. If you are "labeled," or if people pile on and make fun of you for anything that makes you unique, it can be much harder. The desire for acceptance by others dominates. It's a time that can either make or break you. Sadly, for so many, it breaks them.

Breaking can be anything from depression, to drifting away from the love and happiness of earlier years, never to return, or worse. For too many, especially those bullied, it can go as far as suicide. More recently we've seen those hurt to the point of being suicidal, striking out at others by trying to hurt them or kill them. Have we ever considered what role ignoring what we learned in kindergarten, "Treat others the way you want to be treated" has had in our culture today?

I always had the love and support of my mom and dad, my Grandpa Tony, Grandma Iona, and extended family. In terms of peers at 14 and 15, I had none I could trust. I played the trumpet but was not cool. I played golf and was a good bowler, but I was not truly athletic. I just was different. I didn't have the acceptance I so desperately sought. Simply put, life sucked.

In the months prior to April 11, 1991, nasty and untrue rumors were going around about me. I tried to defend, but it never helped the situation. I stopped fighting, and it made it worse. I was in a no-win situation. I was unloved, unwanted and it seemed clear to me that everyone would be better off if I was out of their way.

Everyone else seemed to have it all figured out. I was the hopeless one, the black sheep, the runt of the liter. Adding to the hopelessness was my mom being transferred from working 15 minutes away, to a new store in Binghamton nearly two hours away. Instead of seeing her every night, I would see her only two days a week. She was the only one I could talk to most times as I struggled in my relationship with my dad.

One of the few things I enjoyed was being in the USA Jazz Ensemble, playing trumpet in our high school jazz band. I loved the release. I was making great music, and the great harmonies we made as a band no bullies could stop. Or could they? The spring concert was April 11, 1991. We were the night's highlight, as was customary back then.

I was a 15-year-old sophomore and there were many seniors, including two senior trumpet players. After we played a few songs, it came to individual introductions. We were a band of 22 people in an audience of 800 to 1,000 as most seats in the auditorium's lower level were filled. Obviously, the seniors and more popular kids got the bigger ovations. Rick, our director, in classic form and in high energy turned to us and said, "OK, in that screaming trumpet section we have Rich Lupia…"

At that moment, you could hear a pin drop. Awkward silence. There was no clapping from the crowd. I could see in the crowd from some of the kids' rude and vile gestures towards me. Those few seconds felt like an eternity to me. Next, Rick said, "Well, let's hear it for Chad" (a popular senior trumpet player) and the auditorium erupted with loud applause and a standing ovation from some.

In fairness, I wasn't the only one that got very little respect. There were maybe three others that had a similar lack of ovations. Regardless, it was the breaking point for me. The sum of everything in and out of school that had built up in the prior weeks and months hit me on the stage. I felt like I was publicly humiliated and unwanted by anyone. If no one would clap for me, maybe it was true nobody wanted me. Maybe I would be better off dead? I was at the end of my rope and I just couldn't take it anymore. We all have our breaking point. I was at mine.

After the concert, everyone seemed happy with the performances. I was mad, because I just wanted to be happy like everyone else. I slammed a door hard in the hallway and knocked over two of the seniors I didn't see on the other side. They yelled at me and I yelled back as loud as I could, swearing and pouring out my grief. I hid it from my parents when I got to them because I would get a speech about how I was overreacting instead of empathy for my deep hurt.

I left the school never wanting to go back, but I had to in the morning. I didn't want to go back to what felt like a prison. I went home and retreated to my upstairs room to contemplate the end of my life.

I just wanted to go to sleep and never wake up again. I had considered leaving a short note for them at school to play a song over the speakers at school once I was gone. I was going to just take a ton of sleeping pills and die alone. I felt like my dad didn't understand how deep I was hurt, my grandparents were too old and idealistic to help or relate, and I barely saw mom anymore. After hours of crying and not having the nerve to leave my mom and dad heartbroken that I would be gone, I dropped a cassette into my boom box. It was cued up to my favorite song at the time.

During that song, without question, the "Unseen Hand of God" touched me. An odd thought came to mind that it would be the last time I'd ever hear that song. I also realized for the first time that after just one more day of school, spring break would start, and I didn't have to see "those jerks" as I called them, for nine days. I couldn't explain the rest. I just knew in my head and my heart I wasn't supposed to give up or do anything rash like suicide. I just needed to go to bed. I did and fell asleep right away.

I woke up the next morning, did what I had to, to get through the day, and got home. Things didn't change overnight; I just changed my perspective. I resolved not to give up but to fight on and fight back if necessary. I have never been down that dark road since.

Now it's time for my rant.

There are so many people out there hurting. Not just kids and teens, but adults, too. If you asked, and if people were honest there are a ton of millennials, plenty of us Gen-X'ers and even some baby boomers that still live with the scars and bad memories of what happened to them at this stage of life. It doesn't matter the age or the circumstances, one life is too many to lose to suicide. A worst-case scenario we've seen too much recently is the hurt person taking other's lives because of their hell. How do we stop it? You may not like my answer, but I believe it to be the truth:

Stop valuing things over people. Start looking for the best in people instead of the worst. Stop making fun of things people say or do. We are all different and that is a great thing, not a liability. **If we were all the same, as society tries to make us, there would be no need in the world for YOU.** It's time to start thinking of others before yourself. Stop talking. Start listening. Spend (undistracted) time with those you care about.

Stop gossiping about others. If you don't have anything good to say about anyone or anything, don't say anything. If you have a problem with someone or something they said or did, the Bible gives clear direction about this: Go directly to them, not to 50 other people who can't do anything about it. And above all, stop deriving "joy" in your life by celebrating the sufferings of other people. This is whether you know them or not. There are too many people I know who wake up every day with that as a goal. It's sad.

Never forget you are loved by Jesus Christ, the one and only son of God. There is someone who died for you so that you may have life more abundant on this earth, and eternal life beyond this one. If you believe in God, start living this. If you don't believe in God, you will likely not agree with the last statement. Fair enough and that's your right and choice, as it is mine to believe what I believe. At the very least, there should be no argument with the general "treat others the way you'd like to be treated" Kindergarten teaching prior to bringing God into the conversation.

If we would just stop being jerks to each other, so many problems with broken lives, broken families, broken churches, would not be as serious as they are now.

I can guarantee you someone around you has a deep hurt right now. You could be their hero. Want to change the world? You do it one person and a time. And what are you waiting for? You think you have to say so much and be specially trained, but you don't. Just put the phone down, give a loving and genuine embrace, look them in the eye, actively listen, be quiet and let them talk. You watch what happens. You will mean the world to them for bringing them out of darkness.

I'm sick of seeing people suffer and considering ending their lives. I should have told this story a lot more over the last 28+ years than I have. I'm telling it now and will continue to tell it to encourage people to hold on. It's only a season. Life can turn around just like my life did. Things do get better. When you are at the end of your rope, just hold on. And cry out to God in prayer. You really don't know what's around the bend. Yes, it could be more trouble, but it's only for a time. What if it's meeting "the one"? A big promotion! A nice surprise you didn't expect. Your favorite team having a great season and making a big playoff run! All those things you could miss and so much more.

Things turn around. Big blessings are coming. It's not all smooth sailing. **But you must hold on. Don't. Give. Up.**

Chapter 2
Heart Level

I still had to fight through high school, but things slowly got better. The change of perspective and attitude with me was helping. I still had only a few friends and valued them like gold. I felt lonely at home with mom working so much. I did the best I could but had to power through some incredibly tough days. A few weeks before this day came, I hit another bottom when an intense round of rumors and bullying hit. I was starting to question whether it would ever end.

I've always been one to look on the bright side, most of the time. It was May 1992. The weather was nice, and I didn't have to be trapped inside the house. I could hide out on the golf course. I started working more. While I was doing my best to cope, I was hoping for a breakthrough.

Pete was one of my few friends at the time and was trying to help me through this. Pete was a popular football player for another school, smart and always had the girl's attention. If he was single, it was his own fault! His dad was good friends with my dad for many years. Pete was always a friend to those in need. We had worked together for several months in my first job. As he got to know me, he really felt for me and wanted to do all he could to make life better. He knew all I needed were good friends and a few good breaks.

While working together, he said, "There's this group of friends I hang out with on Wednesday night. You should come along! You'll really like them. Meet me Wednesday night at 7 p.m. at Immanuel Baptist Church in New Hartford".

I descended into the basement of the church and saw this kid just standing there waiting for people. His name was Chad.

He handed me a postcard with a picture of a smiling sun and the words *"Get well soon. You're missed."*

He joked, "Hey… you… you've got to have this to get in otherwise it costs you five dollars!"

I took it with a funny look on my face and thought to myself, "Boy, this is an interesting place, isn't it!" Unsure of what to come, I followed Pete into the meeting hall in the basement.

Naturally, given the rough time in my life to that point, I was guarded and tried not to stand out. I learned very quickly that you can't do that in a well-run youth group. Everyone started hooting and hollering as a completely muscle-bound man with a mustache and a big smile on his face came into the room shouting like he had won the lottery. It was a sight to behold. He said, "Let's hear it for the greatest youth group in the area… the state... the country… the world!!!" Everyone was cheering and clapping as loud as they could as if they really believed it! That's because, they truly did believe it. It was not fake.

His name was Rance and he was the youth pastor. He said, "Welcome to Heart Level, and *as is customary* if you are here for the first time, take four steps out from the wall, turn and say your name, where you're from and who brought you here".

Gulp.

I went numb in fear. In just seconds, I would be in front of 38 kids who had never met me. Given what I went through over the years, I was not hopeful. I looked at Pete and said, *"I don't care how big you are, I don't care you're on the football team, I'm going to kill you!"*

Pete just laughed at me with a big smile saying, "Oh yeah, I forgot to tell you. No big deal. Trust me you'll be alright".

All right? My pulse was racing, adrenaline flowing, and I was about to pass out! I did what was asked. I turned to the 38 strangers and said, "I'm Rich Lupia, I'm from Utica and Pete brought me here I think to embarrass me!"

As I walked back, the ovation from Rance and the 38 was thunderous. It was unlike anything I had experienced to that point in my life, and few since have come close. They were literally screaming at the top of their lungs, clapping, and it was not an act. They were truly happy I was there. I wasn't the geek, dork, ugly one or, "Who is this weird kid" like I was used to hearing. I was accepted. I was loved, and I knew it. For someone longing for love and acceptance, I found my place at 7 p.m. Wednesday May 27, 1992. You don't forget the moment you found hope, love and light after being on the edge of darkness having stared into the abyss of hopelessness.

That night I discovered what true friendship, true love and a personal relationship with Jesus Christ were. It was nothing that was taught to me before. It was everything that was shown to me. It had nothing to do with rules, rituals or what was preached, it was simply the Gospel being lived out in Rance, his leaders and the kids that were there.

I instantly had several friends, real friends that I enjoyed great times with. People wanted to get to know me and wanted to hang out with me. They weren't worried it would ruin their "status" at school. My first girlfriend came from that group. It was not perfect by any means, but it was miles better than anything I had ever experienced or thought even existed.

I began going every Wednesday night. It became the highlight of my week and every time there was a special event to me. My focus at that time was filling the deep hole in my social life and the good friends that wanted to be around me. Week after week, month after month going through the rest of 1992 and into my senior year of high school, this was how I got through.

While I liked what they were teaching about God, it was secondary to the social need I was seeking to fill. What I didn't see yet was God working on my heart to soften me and draw me closer to him. The "Unseen Hand of God" was holding on to me and it was not going to let go. I just didn't know it yet.

Chapter 3
Saved!

Having been to Heart Level and Rance's youth group, I got to know God and the Bible in a way I never had growing up in a different church. For eight months, I asked questions and wondered what the catch was. It seemed too easy. Salvation is a gift from God, not by works, lest anyone should boast. Ephesians 2:8-9. Sometimes it's so simple, we miss it. Many of us tend to overthink things, especially me. When it comes to God, it's simple and spelled out in black and white in the Bible. Accepting it and living it honestly from your heart day after day when you are born sinful and selfish, is "the catch".

We were on a trip for President's Day Weekend 1993. It would take us to Circle C Ranch in Delevan, NY, a Christian camp in the rolling hills an hour south of Buffalo for three days and two nights. We then would go to Rance's old church for an overnight stay, then a Monday morning day trip to Niagara Falls before going home. It was a four-day blockbuster trip for kids and teens. I was so excited to go!

Saturday morning, Feb. 13, 1993 was the first full day there. It was clear and sunny, but bitter cold with a temperature of maybe 15 degrees above zero, not counting the wind chill. There was plenty of snow on the ground. The hills looked painted on, a frosting of white. Little did I know, my sins were about to be washed as white as that snow, and my life would change forever.

It was morning chapel service, and Wes Arum Sr., the founder and owner of Circle C Ranch, was speaking. There were 150 to 200 teens listening. He delivered the Gospel loud and clear, just like Rance had for months in youth group. Something inside of me said this all makes sense now. It's real.

Jesus Christ is real; he is alive, and he died for me on the cross. I needed him because of my own sin, and we all fall short of the glory of God (Romans 3:9).

After the message, Wes asked if anyone would like to come up and give their lives to Jesus and pray for the Holy Spirit to come into our lives. Many Christians call it "praying the prayer" or a "sinners' prayer". So many say it but go back to their own lives and didn't mean it with no change in their lives afterwards.

I walked up. I meant it. And I believe at that moment God the Father drew me to his son, Jesus Christ. It was hard to fight back tears. The sensation was weird, and I just can't explain. It's something you can't imitate or recreate.

We were taken to the back while the rest of the groups went to lunch. Wes talked to us for a few minutes. He made clear the seriousness of what we just did. The excitement was palpable. Wes asked us to tell our leaders that we prayed to receive Jesus Christ.

I went back to the Roy Rogers cabin I was staying in and grabbed a Bible. I started at Psalms 41 and just kept reading. I wanted to know more. It was the first time in my life I had ever felt a desire to read and study God's word. I was somewhere around Psalm 78 when Rance and the other boys found me. They searched for me thinking I was upset, or something was wrong because I didn't go tubing or join the snowball wars outside. I told Rance about going forward with Wes, which he already knew. I told him where I was and shared about the chapters I just read.

He got the biggest smile on his face, and exclaimed "Yeah, the Holy Spirit hit you! That is so awesome man!"

He gave me a giant bear hug and was in tears.

The rest of the vacation was an exciting experience, one of the most fun trips of my life, filled with crazy stories that can only happen in a teen church youth group. Pro Tip: If anyone asks you to eat a whole lemon as fast as you can, just walk away. Trust me on this one! Despite taking that challenge and finding it painful to bite anything for about two days afterwards, I never wanted the trip to end.

Things didn't magically get better, just like they didn't after I was near suicide, but I knew the truth and the truth had set me free. School was different. Life was different. Those close to me noticed the change and started asking me about it.

On April 28, 1993, I gave my testimony to the youth group. They heard about my life to that point, the good, the bad, and the ugly. I testified to them coming to know Jesus as my Lord and savior and thanking everyone for their part in life being better. While I thought it would be well received, I didn't expect a standing ovation. Everyone then gathered around me to pray for me then each person gave me a big hug. I swear that night I had the smallest taste of what Heaven will be like.

With faith, confidence and direction, I finished high school well. The graduation party I thought I'd have maybe 10 people at, I had more than 100. Almost the whole youth group showed up! My dream to be a meteorologist took me 90 miles away to the University at Albany. Life was full of hope, joy and great expectations on what God was going to do next. I was excited to be away from home, but thankful I was only 90 minutes from home. I had always wanted to go to the University of Oklahoma and chase tornadoes for severe storms research (before it was popular like today) but gave up on it because I wanted to be closer to family and friends. I wasn't sure how college life would work out. I also didn't know how much of a challenge living out my faith would be.

Chapter 4
How did I stop?

Those of us who've traveled on the roads of America have all had our share of close calls. Something that could have happened but didn't. Divine intervention. Pure luck. Right place at the right time. Split second gut decision. It can be whatever you want to call it. For me, I'll call Sept. 29, 1995 the day I should have died.

I had been through a lot of ups and downs during freshman and sophomore years at the University at Albany. Academically, I did well the first two years, but was struggling in this fall semester of my junior year. I had found a great church, Grace Fellowship, and became involved with the Christian groups and Bible studies. I needed all the encouragement I could get! I had developed many close friendships that continue to this day. One of them is the editor of this book, my roommate from sophomore year Kevin DeValk, who remembers this story very well.

I was heading from my apartment in suburban Guilderland to the main campus for afternoon classes. I went a different way and didn't know why. I got off at exit 2 off Interstate 90, one of the region's main transportation arteries, and was first in line at the stop light crossing busy Washington Avenue.

The street had several lanes like a highway and traffic was heavy. It was sunny, warm, and beautiful fall day in upstate New York.

I had the windows down in my 1989 Escort, Ford's five speed economy model, which my parents gave me two months prior to this day.

Usually, in heavy traffic, I would take right off when the light turned green. For some reason, this was different.

The next 15 seconds felt like 15 minutes.

When the light turned green, I hesitated for two seconds. I didn't go as fast as I would have. I can't explain that, either. As I was crossing the second half of Washington Avenue, I thought I saw something out of the corner of my eye. I slammed the brakes as hard as I could. Normally you would look at what it was before slamming on the brakes, but if I looked, I would have been dead. What zoomed in front of me, on the eastbound shoulder of Washington Avenue, was another Escort, with four people in it. They flew inches ahead of my stopped car and through the red light at somewhere between 60-70 mph. They sped through the intersection and down the road without slowing down.

I'm sure everyone around me was in disbelief. They probably thought they were about to witness a fatal accident. The person directly behind me never hit my rear bumper, and never beeped his horn. The gentleman yelled out the window to me "I have no idea how you avoided that one". In disbelief, I looked at him for a split second then raised my finger to the sky to point at God. I knew at that very moment it was a miracle I was still alive.

It took me a few minutes to regain composure. While I was mad at the person who nearly took my life, and had a fleeting thought of going after them, I figured there was no way I could catch them. What would I do if I did? I then played out in my head if we had hit. Would I just have been decapitated by the sheer force of the collision? Would I have been punted out of the intersection like a football, tumbling end over end for hundreds of feet? Would I have died instantly from the force snapping my neck and back?

Ultimately, I just went on to class. Shaken. Thankful that I was still alive. Wondering how and why.

There have been many times since that I've remembered this incident and felt like I'm living on borrowed time. Life is precious, and we take for granted when we leave home and hit the road, we have the power, confidence, and training to avoid getting into an accident. You never know what's around the bend. I don't know why God does what He does. I don't understand why bad things happen to good people. I'll never know this side of Heaven. All I can do is try to recognize the moments when I know I've been spared trouble and be thankful for every blessing I am given.

After all these years, I still love to drive. With all the traveling I do, it's easy to take for granted I'll safely get where I'm going. Days like this serve as a humble reminder that at the end of the day, God is in charge, and not me.

Chapter 5
The Struggle

Junior year at the University at Albany was by far the hardest. I struggled through difficult core classes for meteorology, which were math and theory based. I was always better at the operational and practical applications of meteorology, but the theory, equations and derivations drove me nuts. I just didn't get it. Being graded on a curve with a group of curve smashers (smart kids) in your class didn't help. In addition, I was in a lease in an apartment with roommates who went off the deep end. They brought a "friend" up from Long Island to physically assault me, surprising me in my apartment while I was sleeping. I'm thankful nothing happened. This was drama I didn't need. It forced me to move in the middle of the semester.

I appealed to the leader of a ministry on campus who stated he wanted to help people. He could have helped me but chose not to. There was no offer to take me in when he had the ability to, make phone calls to connect me to others who could help, or follow up on how things were going with me. The hypocrisy of this "leader" was stunning. It hurt. I stayed away from his group after that.

One of my favorite passages in the Bible is 1 John 3:17-18 ESV, *"But if anyone has the world's goods and see his brother in need, yet closes his heart against him, how can the love of God abide in him? Little children let us not love in word or talk but in actions and truth."*

With no one able or willing to help, I was left with no choice but to rent a room off campus with strangers, a family that looked at me suspiciously, with money I didn't have. I had to have a home base to finish out the semester. I had just bombed midterms. Plans for my 20th birthday the week prior fell apart. I had mistreated my good friend, Jason, who was in the same program as I and nearly ended our friendship over trivial junk.

Life sucks sometimes. It was then, and I wasn't handling it well. Besides a lot of bad breaks and trials, my treatment of others was not right. I was digging my own grave so to speak. After months of prayer with no good answers because my prayers were selfish, I hit a breakpoint. I was bitter at God. I foolishly thought God was supposed to keep me from hurting like I did before I was saved. Check the Bible. God never promises us easy, smooth and prosperous.

I had slipped down into a false gospel. I was trying to plead with God I was a good person with a good heart and good intentions and that I should have some protection from these trials. University should not be so hard. People should be nicer to me. I should have more of the things I want. Why haven't things worked out the way I wanted them to?

Nearly every Christian I know has slipped into this funk at some point where we are not walking the way we should. If you are there, there is no easy way out. You've got to do the hard work. I'm thankful for a good man at Grace Fellowship that saw my situation and invested himself into me. Read 1 Peter 5 and 1 Corinthians 10, especially verse 13 if you want to know his counsel. Go read it yourself and let God work. For someone who was about to fall away, it was his love, patience, forgiveness and unselfishness that got me to see the truth and end the struggle.

Chapter 6
Mission Accomplished

    While at the University at Albany, I decided severe storms research or teaching was not for me. Being an operational meteorologist, a forecaster, was what I found out I really wanted. Television was the most attractive to me at that time. More and more television stations were bringing on their own meteorologists instead of doing a "rip and read" of what the National Weather Service sent to them. In my hometown TV stations began to use meteorologists in 1993. I had sought to get to know the new meteorologists and they were all very welcoming of me. All were happy to help and encourage me in every way possible. I was allowed two internships for credit, the National Weather Service in Albany which I did that spring, and the internship at my hometown TV station in the summer of 1996.

    The wall. The Chroma key wall, a wall of uniform color, which is usually a color most people don't wear, like a lime green. Anything you wear that's not the wall color, you "key" in front of, making it look like you are standing in front of a projection of a map or graphics. It's all via a computer program. It's a blank wall you are in front of. Monitors on the sides help you see where you are "on the wall". Your left and right are in reverse. You have to master this, talking coherently on the fly and keeping in time as they are talking to you from the control room into your earpiece while all this is going on. It takes a lot of practice, patience and training to perfect. I worked hard "on the wall". In local television in the 1980s and 1990s, it was a big deal and usually only used by meteorologists. Today it is more widely used by news anchors and other talent on more virtual sets.

In doing dozens of practice weathercasts between the real newscasts in the mornings, I go to the point where I was getting better each time. They were very patient with me as I tried to get comfortable and up to speed. I was also making the forecasts and graphics behind the scenes that would go on the air for weathercasts. I did not know at the time they were eyeing me for a "fill-in" role, basically a fourth person on a three-person team, in case someone was on vacation or sick. All I knew was I was making a tape on my final day of my internship. In the business, it was called a "resume tape", or a "demo tape" of you giving your forecasts. Today you email these clips from files you have or from You Tube. Back then, you had to make these tapes on your own and mail them to prospective stations you sought to work at.

The lights were on, the weathercast was ready to go, and they needed a minute to set up to record my tape. We were doing it as if it was a real newscast. At the wall, with a few moments to myself, I took a deep breath and said a prayer, asking God to help me and provide me an opportunity to work in the field.

I had no idea that God would answer almost immediately. That afternoon I got a call, telling me to report to the newsroom at 8 a.m. the next morning. I thought it would be for constructive feedback, a thank you for interning at the station and an invitation to practice more when I was off from school. When I got there to speak to the news director, I heard the start of my dream come true. "I want to hire you."

I have no idea if I held it all inside or not. My professional career had officially begun! I resigned from my job flipping burgers at McDonald's. Less than two days later, at 6:30 a.m. on Thursday Aug. 15, 1996, I was on TV in my hometown doing the weather.

The response was immediate and positive. I was fortunate to be liked by many who were watching, including some who told the station so. Family and friends were all positive in their feedback. It was exciting to live through! It was only supposed to be three days on the air, but an unexpected schedule change meant they needed me for an additional four days.

After seven full days on the air, I was called into office of the general manager, Steve. He wasted no time, offering me the weekend weather job on a permanent basis. I was literally, living the dream.

But I still needed the degree to keep the dream. I was taking 17 credit hours that fall and needed 17 more in the spring to graduate officially become a meteorologist. There was a ton of work ahead. Over the next nine months, I had a grand total of 12 days off, including all weekends and holidays. Six of that was one vacation in March. The other six days were spread out across the calendar randomly. I worked, even if I was tired and sick. Yes at 21 years old, you can and should work like that. It's biblical to work hard for God and run with the goal to win the prize (Philippians 2). To paraphrase a Proverb, if you don't work, you don't eat. One of the ways I was able to survive was because I was doing work I always wanted to do. I was living my passion and using the gifts I knew God gave me.

That zone is hard to find and hard to maintain, but you should never stop seeking it. That passion that can only come from God will carry you places you never thought you would go, to things you never thought you could go through. It was that passion that carried me through the rest of those classes at Albany. It got me through the last day of finals, the hardest final in the hardest class. I was barely passing and needed my professor to correct the final in front of me so I knew if I would walk at graduation two days later. I made it. I finally got the degree I had sought all my life.

Two weeks later I received a promotion as the chief had moved to another job and was promoted to the next step which was full-time morning meteorologist. I got to be a part of the first team to bring expanded morning news and weather at our station. Four years after graduating high school I accomplished for all to see, the dream I had always dreamed.

It seems like happily ever after should be the next line in this story. It's not. Life is not a fairy tale. There may be seasons and moments it is like that. Not to say I didn't have great times and incredible experiences, but it wasn't every day. Sometimes it was the fault of others. Sometimes it was bad breaks. But the majority of the time, the problems I ran into in the coming months and years were of my own making.

Chapter 7
The waiting and more struggling

Waiting and more struggling is how you would best describe the first years of my working life after leaving school.

My parents, both natives of upstate New York, had moved to Henderson, Nevada. My mom got a great job there. I was left behind in Utica to live in the house I grew up in while it was being sold. They thought I would move away at the first opportunity, and that was my goal at the time. As an only child, this was a tough one for me. Great, I had an awesome place to vacation, but not so great on a day to day basis when they are 2,500 miles away and you are alone to deal with things in your life that come up when you are first on your own.

My combination of high energy and enthusiasm was very well-received by the community that watched me on TV. I always tried to look on the bright side and had confidence in my work. Where this trait was a liability was the new world of office politics, egos (a big thing for many on TV), and games at work. I opened my mouth one too many times, on one too many occasions. A lot of it was over trivial stuff and my pride. In a church or in a family, these things usually get worked out for the best over time as you learn and grow. This doesn't always happen in the professional world and was the case here.

I became a leader in my old youth group at Immanuel Baptist. It was awesome to give back of my time and energy to the younger kids, which I had such a tender heart for having been through my struggles at that age. It was great hanging out with the kids, getting to know them, and trying to help them through when they needed help. I had good friendships with the other leaders, but I strained them over time. I leaned on the leaders too hard to fill the void of loneliness I had from my parents leaving and not many people my age around the church or in the area at that time. It became more about me than serving and that was wrong.

And then there was waiting for my soulmate. That was the worst. The number of young women I liked, took an interest in, pursued, and failed was embarrassingly high. I was always a nice guy, faithful and loyal, and had a deep desire to settle down and start a family of my own. I wasn't looking just for a good time, but for someone I could share a life with. Here I was failing too. I was trying too hard sometimes. Other times I was too scared to make a move. There were moments I kept going with those that made clear their interest in me was not the same. On the flip side, some were being genuinely nice to me and made clear interest, and I didn't respond to the same level. I made so many mistakes and misread so many situations.

What do all the above situations I was dealing with between 1997 and 2000 have in common? Among many things, self-focus. I was basing my life more off feelings and the opinions of others rather than who I am as a new creation in Jesus Christ. I was not studying the Bible and praying like I should. As a Christian I would talk about my faith, but the actions were lacking. The combinations of my own mistakes and bullying from others, caused a major lack of self-confidence. At times I would just freeze in fear. I was playing right into the hands of the Devil with those two choice weapons - doubt and fear.

Read James 1:5-8, especially verse 8. That was me more days than not between 1997 and 2000; unstable in all I did.

What started during the winter of 2000 and lasted for several months was a "perfect storm". It came from all sides. First it started with issues at my job, and things that had been blown way out of proportion. Then it was criticism from work and everyone else I knew that I was starting to put too much weight on. Rumors and gossip flew everywhere from work, to church to the community. Relationships were falling apart. Dates were going bad. I hid it well on TV, most of the time.

One person God was using in my life to help me through this season was Mark Enjem. We met in 1997 working out at a local gym. I would work out in the late afternoons and Mark would be there after he got done with work. He knew me as the weatherman. I knew him as the young, bright and sometimes humorous face on our television station commercials. Mark was the face and voice of Enjem's, a fourth-generation family business in the region since 1917 (and still today). As we worked out and talked through the late 1990s, we became good friends. We were both believers in Christ with similar life goals: Find a good Godly woman, marry her, you'll be happy then, raise a family, work hard, and pass it on to the next generation.

It was during those stormy times in the winter, spring and summer of 2000 we spent as much time together as we could. We took as many road trips as we could. We had so many talks from lunch after I got out of work. We would go and hang out at his apartment or mine whenever we could. We both were trying to help each other through the struggles we were facing. We both prayed a lot. Mark has always been a great friend, but during this time, I honestly don't know what I would have done without him.

I left my role volunteering with the youth group and Immanuel Baptist. I gave up on some relationships, messed up with others, grew callous and cynical to everyone around me, and was looking for any escape.

By this point I had realized I messed things up and knew I had to do it better if given another chance. I wanted to quit my job and leave central New York. I simply wanted to hit the reset button and start over again. I was determined not to screw things up so bad if I was given another chance. A second chance to make things right.

Chapter 8
El Capitan and Half Dome

Las Vegas and the Desert Southwest had become my second home. Any opportunity to take time off and catch a flight out west to get away from the hot mess that was my life at that time, I took it. Besides my parents, other family and their friends who liked me a lot, no one else knew me out there. There was no drama. Nothing to mess up.

During those trips my parents and I would take off on road trips from Las Vegas to explore the great National Parks and natural wonders in this part of the world. There are so many hidden gems. The stunning natural beauty is something I love so much and miss living back east. If you've never been west of the Rockies, you would not understand.

In early September 2000, I took a desperately needed 10-day trip out west to see mom and dad. This trip, we made plans to explore Sequoia National Park and Yosemite National Park. It's a long road trip from Las Vegas but such a neat experience going from microclimate to microclimate, mountain ranges, to valleys, plateaus and gorges.

Sept. 6, 2000 was the day we made it to the Yosemite Valley and I first laid my eyes on El Capitan, Half Dome and the Sierra Nevada's. It was one of the most breathtaking scenes I had ever seen. I certainly understood at that moment why that park was so crowded!

The scene brought into focus the presence of God and it brought me to a breaking point in my life. The weight of everything that had happened in the three years since graduation and my parents moving out west, hit me there.

I was absorbing the stunning scenery before me and just simply broke down. I had enough of trying to do it my way, fight God or just sit impatiently like a little child waiting for a toy or for candy. I felt I had ruined everything I had. I felt no one would forgive me or give me a second chance if I tried to make amends. I just wanted to start over. Where was the reset button?

It was my moment before God to confess my desperate need for him to take control of my life in a way I had not let him before, even as a Christian.

And it was here after pouring this all out unexpectedly over the course of a few minutes that I lifted a prayer to God. The prayer was something like this: *"God all I want for my 25th Birthday is a brand-new life. I just want a new job. A new place to live. I just want to start over again. I'm sorry I messed things up so bad. Please give me another chance to start over again."*

I felt a peace that something was going to happen. I just knew things were not going to be messed up forever.

How did God answer? Keep reading!

Chapter 9
Meeting Amy

I cried when I returned home from Yosemite and Las Vegas on Sept 10. I hated coming back east, facing work and the situations I left behind. I wanted to go back out west so bad because my parents were there, natural beauty was there, and problems were not there. I was at that point I would do just about anything to leave upstate New York.

I was very quiet that week at work. I did my work, avoided any unnecessary contact, and got myself out of there. The week seemed to pass so slowly. Finally, the weekend arrived.

Saturday morning Sept. 16, 2000, Mark Enjem received a call from an old friend from a Bible study he used to go to. Her name was Amy Lawrence, a beautiful, quiet and modest young woman who ultimately had the same goals as Mark and I. Amy knew this. She was also single and struggling to be patient with God's plan for her life. Amy had called to ask if Mark was single and if he'd like to go out on a date. At that time, Mark had a girlfriend. In that moment, as any best friend and wingman would, he turned it around. Mark told her, "But I know somebody that's interested in getting to know you". Amy listened as Mark told her about me and asked if he could give me her number. She agreed. The moment he hung up, guess what he did?

My phone rang, and it was Mark. I was hoping he was calling to let me know we could get together and do something that day. He immediately said, I can't get together this weekend, but "I know someone that's interested in getting to know you". He then told me about Amy and gave me her number. She was expecting my call, so I did. After all the women I had sought or had been introduced to, I went in with no expectations anything would happen.

Amy sounded very pleasant and sweet. I asked if there was a time, we could get together later that day or on Sunday. She let me know she was going out of town for a wedding then had church and plans with her family on Sunday, meaning we couldn't get together until Monday Night after she got out of work at 6 p.m.

Immediately I was thinking this was going to be just like every other blind date setup I had over the last three years. I was hoping it wouldn't end up in disaster. With the fact that I had to wait almost three days just to meet, *I honestly thought she really didn't want to get to know me*. Mark was just trying to keep me from leaving and figured a nice girl in my life could keep me around town.

Monday Sept. 18, 2000 came, a sunny and warm late summer day, 80 degrees and bright sunshine. I worked my morning and noon weathercasts then did what I did most afternoons after work: Take a nap! I got up after a few hours and got ready to meet Amy Lawrence, just after 6 p.m. for dinner.

I had no idea what she looked like. I was relieved when I saw her that it wasn't like some of the crazy setups I had in the past. She was beautiful with a great smile and a little shorter than me. She looked happy to see me, which is always a good sign! I held the door for her, and inside we went to enjoy our evening together.

As was typical, being on TV, many people recognized me. Amy was captivated by that and thought it was quite funny. I focused on being a gentleman, asking questions to get to know her, not going on too much about me, and just trying to be the nice guy I was at heart. Maybe the fact that I was not trying too hard, like I did in the past, helped me make a good impression. After a great dinner and conversation, Amy didn't want the night to end. It was 8 p.m. and I didn't want to be out too late since I needed to be up at 3 a.m. to go to work the next morning. She was sad that I wouldn't go out for coffee and more conversation afterwards.

We left each other with a hug then got into our cars to drive home. So often in my life the nice girls I met and wanted to be around lived so far away. Now I had one so close by, literally two blocks from my apartment. Walking distance!

Little did I know during those two hours, Amy had experienced what she always dreamed about. I was the one she was looking for. She knew right away. As for me, after meeting so many women, I've learned it's what you don't see that's most important about a person. This is especially true in a potential mate. The world focuses on the beauty, the love and passion part of relationships while ignoring the heart and character of a person. I had met a beautiful person inside and out that fateful night. I wanted to get to know her. I met my wife without even knowing it.

God answered the prayer!

Chapter 10
The choice

Over the next few days, Amy and I tried to spend as much time as possible outside of work. We enjoyed being with each other. I was starting to really like her, which conflicted with the reality of what I wanted to do with my career and my life. I did not want to hurt her. As Amy learned of this and my desire to leave the area, she knew she had to tell me how she really felt.

It was less than two weeks after we met. We were sitting down, and this quiet and shy woman got a boldness to say what must have been the scariest words for her to say in her life.

"I think you are the one."

I was not expecting this at all. I still remember the shock as she told me this. I was very flattered as I really liked her too. I honestly told her I didn't feel the same way yet, but I made darn sure she knew that because I didn't feel that way at that moment did not mean that I did not want to be with her.

I had an interview for a job in Pensacola, over Columbus Day Weekend. I thought at the time that this was where I was going. Amy was praying it would fall through. The interview went great, but I had angst I just couldn't explain. As much as it seemed right, there was no peace.

Though I loved the area and the people I could be working with, when I got on the plane and was flying out of Pensacola, I just knew I wasn't coming back. It was certain. The whole plane ride home I just couldn't explain it. The overwhelming feeling that can only be explained as the

"Unseen Hand of God". The Pensacola job was not the one for me. Amy was the one for me and I needed to stay put where I was. It made no sense because I felt all things were beyond repair back home in Utica. But God was about to do something amazing.

After the noon news on a rainy Oct. 18th I left work to meet Amy for lunch at our favorite lunch place next to where she worked, the old Peppy's Pizza. Amy was very concerned with what was happening with me at work and we spent her lunch break talking about everything. Work had found out I interviewed down south and was ready to bail. I thought for sure they would say "good" and hasten the end, but they did something inconceivable a few short months before: They tried to convince me to stay.

Amy and I both prayed at the table that God would make His will clear to us. The answer was immediate. I had all the peace in the world about stopping the job search, staying where I was at, seeing everything through with Amy and sticking it out to rebuild things at work. I left on that rainy day to go home and nap while she went back to work. Driving home and looking around I knew God made clear that day that Utica was home, things would work out, and Amy and I were where we needed to be.

Amy and I fell deeply in love shortly after that. Things at work got better. When the offer did eventually come from Pensacola several weeks later, I declined. They counter offered again, and I declined again. For my career, it was a stupid move. I had a clear and strong offer to move up to a much larger market. But life is not all about work. What good is a big job in a much bigger market with lots of sunshine and no one special to share it with? It was a step of faith that the "Unseen Hand of God", I believe, moved me towards.

Chapter 11
The dream comes true

I knew shortly after this time that Amy was the one. The fact she came with me to Nevada to see my mom and dad, spending a week with me in southern Nevada just prior to Christmas 2000, was so overwhelming to me. When I put her on the plane heading back to New York on Dec. 23rd, I felt so empty. I wanted to be with my mom and dad for Christmas like I had planned before I met Amy, but I felt like a part of me was missing. Looking back now, it was leaving McCarran Airport that cool, sunny day before Christmas Eve that I knew without a doubt she would be my wife. It took me a lot longer than her to figure it out, but I got the memo.

With the New Year, you'd think that Valentine's Day would have been the best time to propose. I didn't want to be predictable or bend to commercialized pressure. Amy and I have never been like that when it comes to expressing our love. It has been in the everyday and the little things, not the big splash events and expectations the world demands. We did enjoy a sweet Valentine's Day, but we were not worried. We were on our own timeline. We were "ring shopping" at the time and we both knew the other was not going anywhere.

Amy's dad died tragically when she was two years old, so I had no father to ask for a blessing. On Sunday, Feb. 25, 2001, I asked her mom, Nancy (Mamwah). The blessing was given without hesitation and we celebrated a great day together!

Our first test as a couple came the night before the proposal, Friday March 2. I had planned to take her to Chittenango Falls, where we went for a hike on one of our first dates. In winter it was sure to be quiet but beautiful. She came over the night before. I was tired and not feeling well. The issue was so trivial I don't even remember to this day what we both got upset, but it was our first actual argument. We left each other hurt that night. Amy thought she had blown it with me, and I would leave. I thought I had blown it with her, and she would leave me. Alone in our apartments, we were scared, crying and praying for what was to come, hoping it would be a happily ever after together.

The next morning, I showed up at her place with flowers in hand, a heartfelt card, a sincere apology and asking that we would still spend the day together. She was so happy and relieved and said yes. And so, we were off for "a ride." I knew where, but she didn't.

Saturday March 3 was breezy and cold with lake effect snow. I know, only a meteorologist like me would remember details like that! No breaks in the clouds, none forecasted, and temperatures were in the low 20's. About 18" of snow was on the ground. Typical of Upstate New York on the first weekend of March. We arrived in Chittenango Falls to find, to our surprise, *people*! I wanted a quiet place, beautiful and alone with her. I wanted no witnesses or to make a spectacle. Everywhere we go, people were there and would not leave. I grew impatient and Amy couldn't understand why I was upset. We then trudged into the 18" snowpack down the slopes of the picnic area to a view of the icy falls out of sight of the people there at the top.

Amy went to zip up my Columbia jacket and broke the zipper! She laughed and shook her head and said, "I'm sorry I'm constantly breaking things!" At that moment, I reached into the inside pocket and said emphatically, "Hopefully, you won't break this". I dropped to one knee and then I couldn't speak. I was cold, scared and in shock that I was proposing to her. She looked in awe at the ring but was waiting for me to say something. I said dumbly, "Well?" To which she replied, "Well, aren't you going to ask me"? I said, "Amy will you marry me?"

She said yes!

We were so happy and on cloud nine! The joy was overwhelming. I honestly don't remember feeling my cold wet boots or wet jeans from standing in the snow. We skipped and hopped; it felt like we were floating, back up the hill to my car! We get into the car and Amy took her glove off to take a closer look at the ring. She was in awe.

In one incredible moment that could not have been timed more perfectly, the sun penetrated the clouds, hit the ring and dazzled an indescribable show of light through the car. It is nothing we've ever seen or been able to duplicate since. That moment, we felt the "Unseen Hand of God" on us. We were meant to be together, forever and for always. It literally took our breath away.

As we left Chittenango - to head for her friend Suzann's in Syracuse to announce and celebrate our engagement, the clouds rolled away at sunset to reveal an incredible sky as we looked down on the lights of Syracuse driving into the city. That picture is still in my mind to this day. I haven't seen anything like that since.

The proposal and the rest of that day were just perfect. We all decided to go to a steak dinner at Delmonico's, talk about wedding plans, and talking about our future with excitement!

A beautiful engagement followed over the spring and summer of 2001. If there was ever a time in my life I could bottle up and take with me, this period would have been it. We were constantly going on dates, exploring different places together, and just so happy to be together. Everywhere we went, even familiar places, seemed so much better and right because we were together. We were in love, and thankful to God.

We were married on Sept. 8, 2001 on a warm, sunny day in the presence of nearly 300 of our family and friends. It was the best day, best celebration and best party of our lives. I would liken it to an out of body experience. You go to so many weddings and one day, it's yours! It was truly a day you wanted to remember forever and relive forever. That day and the days leading up to it were so special.

The morning after our wedding, we boarded the plane for Hawaii. Six days in Maui, one day at Waikiki, and the chance to go to Pearl Harbor to pay our respects to those who gave their lives for our country. We had so many plans. After a full day of travel on the 9th and being jet lagged on the 10th, we woke up for breakfast on Tuesday morning Sept. 11, 2001. I turned on the local news and it took me a few minutes to comprehend what was going on. Even after I did, I couldn't believe it.

Because of the time change with Hawaii, six hours behind the east coast, we didn't see it live, like most of the country. It was 6:30 a.m. when I turned the TV on - about 90 minutes after the second of New York City's two World Trade Center towers, hit by hijacked airplanes, came down.

We wanted to return home so bad. We were shocked, filled with sadness, and unsure of what the future would bring. It's impossible to enjoy paradise when you are scared to death, thousands of your fellow citizens were killed and not knowing what was going to happen next. We were told initially we could be stranded in Hawaii for weeks (with a significant and unknown financial burden). We got lucky in the fact that when flights resumed our initial reservations did not get scrubbed. The one place I didn't get to go to, in paying my respects to my Grandpa's generation that fought for our country in WWII, was Pearl Harbor. It was still shut down as we flew out, so we only caught a glimpse from the plane as we took off from Honolulu. I hope one day we will get the chance to go back.

We returned home, and to work, beginning our life together as husband and wife. We made it a point to enjoy every moment, every time with friends and family, every trip, every day. Pray often. Love recklessly. Be thankful. We wanted to raise a family. We were developing new dreams. The events of 9/11 prompted us to travel as often as we could when we had the time and resources to do so. Our travels took us to friends and family, simply spending time together. The games, the meals being out together, the walks to beautiful vistas, and great conversation. Encouraging each other. Those trips in that first year were so special. What I had wished for so hard for most of my life was happening.

It was all worth the wait.

Chapter 12
Never the same

About a year after we were married, we found out that Amy was pregnant. We had just put in an offer on our first house, a small three-bedroom one bath ranch home with a finished basement 10 minutes north of Utica in Barneveld. It was an exciting time; we were moving in and it seemed life was coming together about as picture perfect as you would want.

I had wanted to be a dad, but I was scared. I was taken constantly to the baby sections of stores and had no idea what to do with all this baby stuff! We went to the doctor for all the prenatal appointments, ultrasounds, and tests. Overwhelmed, I was! Amy kept reassuring me I would be just fine. She was living a dream herself of being able to bear a child. Having love and encouragement helped get me through my fears and doubts.

We found out over the holidays that we would have a boy. I was happy but Amy was sad. She wanted a girl so bad because she came from a family of all girls. The men had passed on long before I met her, including her dad. We were hoping for two or three children ultimately, with this being the "big brother". When we found out it would be a boy, we decided on the name Zachary, meaning "Gift from God".

Amy gained a lot of weight during the pregnancy. She developed back pain, had trouble eating and had trouble sleeping in those last months. The fact the winter of 2002-03 was a particularly snowy, cold and harsh winter even by Upstate NY standards didn't help. Spring eventually came and so did Amy's due date of April 29th. It became clear Zachary (or "Zack") was not coming out on his own. No contractions. No dropping. Amy's belly was big. Adding to the pressure of just wanting the boy out, my parents flew in from Las Vegas for a two week "vacation" to meet their first grandson. Most of that time was spent waiting for the day.

The decision was made to induce on May 7th. We naturally thought this would be the day. They gave her every drug known to man and nothing worked. It stretched into May 8th, my dad's birthday, and their final full day with us. Still nothing worked. By afternoon we were all impatient, weary and concerned. They decided to do the C-section before night came.

It's truly a miracle, the modern medicine and health care we have. What God can do through doctors, nurses and specialists is incredible. There isn't much more you can say about that. And I got to watch it all happen. Through the Lamaze training I knew what I was in for and what I would see. It's one thing to see it on video or hear people talk about it. It is quite the other to see it happen in person. This is especially true if it's your own wife and you see your own child being pulled out of her belly. I was calm but captivated. I was almost numb as I watched the doctors take Zachary out of Amy's belly; hear him cry for the first time then hear my wife cry out *"Thank you Jesus!"*

Once you become a dad, life is never the same again. And that's a good thing. It's something you just need to experience to know and appreciate how it changes everything in your life. I was way more selfish as a person, especially as an only child. After Zachary was born, a lot of that vanished, and it started on that fateful day.

It's one thing to love and care for your spouse. It's a whole new ballgame when your baby depends on you for everything. I realized how unqualified I was to be a dad and leader of a family. The only way I was going to get through this without hurting this precious child, and/or my precious wife, and/or myself, was by admitting I could not do this on my own. I needed God to help me. I needed to follow God and his teachings in the Bible if I was going to be a good dad.

I don't know what I would do without good friends and family around to help and encourage me to do what I knew I needed to do. Those first weeks seemed like forever. Then the weeks turned into months and the next thing I know he's a year old.

God was working on me, one area at a time. I was not only growing closer in my relationship with Jesus through this time, but to my wife and to this precious boy Zachary. It was nothing I had imagined, but more than I could have ever dreamed.

Chapter 13
Hail of change

Not long after Zack's first birthday, the winds of change had started to blow. I knew things were going to change at work that summer of 2004 because of new ownership coming in. I had recently moved to doing the main newscasts at 5, 6, 10 and 11 p.m. as the previous meteorologist in that shift left for another market. There were a lot of things happening behind the scenes at that time that made us all less certain of the future.

I had started looking for work in my field anywhere in the country. We put the house up for sale. This uncertainty was compounded by the fact my young mistakes professionally were starting to haunt me. This included turning down promising opportunities in years prior to move to other markets, thinking they'd be there when I wanted them. That was not the case. Also, I was terrible at networking. It was awkward for me then and deep down I felt so stupid trying to make conversation. The issues at work over the previous years left me feeling unqualified and out of my league. I had confidence on the air and in my forecasting but had a major crisis of confidence with networking and dealing with other personalities. It was the part of the business I hated most.

The job search went slow and the house sold quicker than I thought, so we had to move back into an apartment, pocket the cash, and wait for the next step. We had to give our dog to friends as every apartment we sought had strict no pet policies. The stress was building. There was more than me to think about. I had not only Amy, but Zack. He was walking now.

We came to the difficult conclusion our future was elsewhere. We'd be leaving all our family and friends behind. It was time to get serious about what to do. In February 2005, we took an 11-day, 4,000-mile trip to check out areas throughout the Southeast where we might want to live. Florida. Georgia. Alabama. Tennessee. North or South Carolina. Besides honestly evaluating places like Huntsville, Nashville and Atlanta, we went to Florida first to see my Grandma Iona. She moved to Cocoa Beach to live with her son a few years after my Grandpa passed away. I had not seen her in years, and she was in failing health. She also never met her great grandson, Zachary. She needed to meet him, and I needed to say goodbye to the woman who meant so much to me growing up. She was always so beautiful, so sweet and so supportive of me just like Grandpa was. I knew leaving Cocoa that was it and it would be sad. She did pass away a few years later.

During the trip, Amy and I prayed over where God would bring us next and asked him to open the doors. The way the prayer was answered was different than we expected. We ended the trip in Atlanta with Amy's close friend, Cindy. We went to church that Sunday with the sermon given by the great Dr. Charles Stanley. The sermon was "Where is your Faith?" Is it a restless faith, a reaching faith or a resting faith? Pouring through scripture and the promises of God, you know the answer is a resting faith. God has got this. It's already done!

The one thing I knew for sure at that point was that I wasn't there. I was so anxious and not even at reaching (or striving) … but restless. Do you remember a few chapters ago? Here I was right back at the same place, but because of a different situation. The bottom line was my lack of faith. This lack of faith is powered by fear and doubt. Just like when I struggled before meeting Amy in the previous chapters.

James 1:6-8 (ESV) was where I was: *But let him ask in faith, with no doubting, for the one who doubts is like a wave of the sea that is driven and tossed by the wind. For that person must not suppose that he will receive anything from the Lord; he is a double-minded man, unstable in all his ways.*

Among other scriptures, Proverbs 3:5-8 (ESV) was where I needed to be: *Trust in the LORD with all your heart, and do not lean on your own understanding. In all your ways acknowledge him, and he will make straight your paths. Be not wise in your own eyes; fear the LORD AND turn away from evil. It will be healing to your flesh[1] and refreshment to your bones.*

I started to realize, yet again, I needed to give control to God. While I did do better after the events of 2000, in general for the first 12 years as a Christian, I was very much wanting to do what I always wanted and fit God into it. It was wrong. I knew I had to be ready to let go of my lifelong dream to work through my career as a meteorologist on TV. That faith was tested as we left Atlanta in rush hour traffic the next afternoon,

We were in the thick of the mess on the perimeter, I-275, when my cell phone rang. I didn't recognize the number. I took the call. It was a news director from a TV station out west that I did not apply to. She asked if I was Rich Lupia and I said yes. For the next two minutes, she proceeded to praise me up and down for how good I was on the air, how polished and experienced I was. The next statement blew me away and nearly got me into an accident in the stop and go traffic: *"After reviewing 300 candidates you were head and shoulders above the rest and we would be honored for you to come to our city and be our next chief meteorologist."*

I thought it was the moment I was praying for months to hear. Instantly the thought of being out west in the mountains, within a day's drive of Las Vegas and with a chance for us to plant our family and start a new life was so invigorating. It was getting real, real fast. But it was a smaller market. It was not Denver, Salt Lake, or Boise calling and I knew the money might not be there. I was hoping it would be just enough to live on.

And that's where we went to the next thing, the compensation. She asked what range I was looking to be in.

Knowing small markets have small budgets and regretting I turned down previous offers, I went against conventional wisdom and lowballed myself. A lot - five figures worth of lowballing. I just wanted to go and put my faith that God would somehow work it out. God already knew there was no way. Even after cutting myself short to move to a place where I wanted to go, there was no way I could take a 50% pay cut. Not with a wife and child to support. Simply put, I wouldn't be able to afford to live there even at a most basic level. They were bummed and said there was no way they could negotiate; the budget was set and that was all they could afford.

We ended the conversation cordially. Zack was asleep. Amy was stunned. And I was pinned in Atlanta traffic trying to get our long 17-hour drive home underway. We had a line of severe thunderstorms coming at us if didn't make it to Chattanooga, TN in time. We did get out of the traffic eventually, but the storms caught us around Dalton, GA. We got crushed with golf ball sized hail and 70+ MPH winds which literally blew us off I-75. It did damage to our SUV! The winds of change literally and figuratively became a *hail of change*.

After that harrowing experience which scared us to death, we just kept driving into the night. We planned to stop off for the night at a hotel to sleep, but Amy and I just kept talking and praying. I couldn't sleep knowing life was about to change and the only thing I had to hold on to was God, my wife and son. I drove all night. We reached Harrisburg, just after 6 a.m. At that point I needed a short nap and a sandwich after waking back up. By noon we pulled into the driveway and everything felt different. I knew in my heart I would be off the air soon. I knew I would be moving on to new work and a new city soon. I just knew. And I just had to have faith God was allowing this to happen for a reason I did not understand.

I retooled the resume away from weather and TV jobs that wouldn't pay the bills. Within days, I had interviews and calls back. The answer was clear to change career paths with my transferable skills and push for a new career. I put my faith and trust in God for what was next. Reaching faith. That was how February 2005 ended.

The next month, I got offers from Las Vegas. In April 2005, the final offer came from Las Vegas from the same company my mom worked for, which I accepted. It was time to say goodbye to my hometown. The goodbyes were tear-filled. Bidding goodbye to Amy's mom, sisters and nieces was heartbreaking. I was leaving as my best friend finally met his soul mate, and months away from him getting married, made me feel like a rotten best friend. Mark was there for me when I needed him. When he needed me, I was moving out.

We left after the 6 p.m. news that Friday April 29th with the SUV fully packed. We grabbed two pizzas from O'Scugnizzo's then hit the Thruway and headed west, into the sunset. I decided not to look back in the rear-view mirror at all until almost Buffalo, three hours into the trip. After driving all night, we spent the whole next day driving across the Midwest and into the Great Plains. By Nebraska, we had had enough and got a hotel for the night.

We started early on May 1 and got to the Rockies in good time. It was my first time ever on I-70 from Denver to Grand Junction, over the Continental Divide. That is the most amazing drive in the world to me. If you never have driven that 250-mile stretch of interstate highway, it's worth it. By the deserts of Utah, we were wearing down but still tried to push on to make Las Vegas without another night in a hotel. Just before midnight after many driver switches, we arrived.

As we drove into the Las Vegas Valley and the bright lights of the strip, I freaked out. I said to myself *"What the heck did I just do?"* At that moment I thought I had just made the biggest mistake of my life. I didn't understand but God did. The "Unseen Hand of God" was on me. Easy to say looking back now, but hard to believe then. The times you must walk by faith you'll do crazy things you never thought you would.

Chapter 14
What's happening to Amy?

We had been in Las Vegas nearly two years. We had stayed several months more with my parents than we had planned. When we were able to rent a home in the beautiful Seven Hills neighborhood, it was incredible. We had a sweeping view of the Las Vegas Strip and the mountains in the distance. I landed a good job at a local media company in sales and marketing. Amy had gone back to work as a pharmacy technician. Zack was almost four, was so in love with trains, and was enrolled in preschool. We were living the life of what was a typical young family - kid in school, with both parents working. Life was on cruise control, but that was about to end.

Amy went away on a ladies' retreat with our church up to St. George, Utah during the last few days in April. I had Zack for the weekend. No problem. Then, she called. Her back had gone out and she didn't know what was going on. She was in such excruciating pain; she could barely talk and couldn't drive. A friend drove her back to our house. Suddenly my wife went from happy and active to nearly paralyzed in pain in just 48 hours. I now had to take care of her and Zack and work full-time. And I had absolutely no idea how to help ease her pain.

Two weeks of doctor and chiropractor visits revealed sciatica and a spine with disks that were degenerating rapidly. She had to be so careful during recovery. She couldn't do anything major and she couldn't pick up Zack. We made it to Mother's Day, and she was better, good enough to enjoy our first day in several weeks. The next morning, we both had to go back to work and Zack had preschool. I watched her bend down to pick up a train track off the floor. Nothing major, no weight, a simple move. Bam. That was it.

Two and a half weeks of progress was gone in a moment. She was screaming and crying in pain. I scrambled to take care of Zack and called in sick to take care of Amy. All the doctors wanted to do was prescribe pills for the pain - hydrocodone and ibuprofen. Rest a few weeks and you'll be fine. Sure, right! We did as we were told, and after nine painful days, with her in bed and no improvement, she went, in desperation, to the emergency room.

Amy got a CAT scan. There was nothing we didn't already know about her back and discs, but it revealed a golf ball-sized shadow by her ovaries. She was sent for further tests. For her pain, she was prescribed Tramadol. Over the coming weeks, her pain did get better, but only because of the pills. When she didn't take them, major withdrawal symptoms set in almost immediately. Zack started to act out, mad and not understanding what was happening with his mom. Others questioned her condition as an "act" and whispered in my ear that maybe I should move on without her. Everything was falling apart. And since I was not having faith in the trial and walking with God like I should have, I believed the junk.

While Amy loved me through it all and was all in with me, I wasn't all in with her. I doubted. I went back to the scared man of years before and started losing my way. When Amy needed me the most, I was at my worst. I became impatient and started thinking of me first. I wanted out of the nightmare, and since Amy just wanted to be back in New York with her sisters and her mom, I sent her back home to her family to recover there. I wondered what the future would hold. Would she recover? Would I give up? Would she want to stay home and not come back to Las Vegas? Was this it?

At this point in my marriage, I was an unsupportive and bad husband. After about a week of me wondering what I should do being alone with Zack in southern Nevada and Amy being home with her family, our pastor from back home interceded. He let me have it, lovingly, and I deserved it.

Shortly into the conversation he said, *"How do you think you are going to draw closer to each other and work things out when you are 2,500 miles away"*? He reminded me of my vows, which I needed to be, and poured scripture into me of what I needed to do. Many men would have looked at it as a slam session, shut down and give up. I didn't. I knew our pastor was a God loving man and an incredible preacher. I knew at heart he wanted the best for us.

I had my lifeline and my chance to begin again. I begged forgiveness for how I was, pledged to walk with God in faith and not fear, and asked Amy to come home as soon as she could. Everything changed from that moment on, July 2, 2007.

Over the next 11 days we would talk constantly on the phone, our conversations growing sweeter as I manned up and started to become the husband she needed. We encouraged each other, started to laugh and dream again. We got back to the point we were at before: We couldn't stand to be away from each other.

On July 13, 2007 we reunited in Las Vegas and could barely keep our hands off each other. We just kept saying "I love you" to each other and pledged to be all in, no matter what. I promised her I'd never go back to the place of doubt ever again in our marriage. She forgave me, and our love was reborn. It was a sweet thing! She had stopped taking the Tramadol and survived the withdrawal symptoms. Her back was better, and she was as close to normal as she had been in almost three months. She experienced emotional healing while she was in New York with her mom and sisters. Things had finally turned back around.

After being apart for 17 days, the longest stretch ever since we met, it looked like everything would be smooth sailing ahead. That only lasted four days.

Chapter 15
Cancer and the prediction

The results of all those tests Amy took prior to going home to central New York had not come back yet. Just four days after coming home and with us looking forward to life again, she got the call that devastated her.

"You have ovarian cancer."

We made an oncology appointment and were told Amy needed to have surgery soon. It didn't take much research for me to realize that this was not good. At that time, those diagnosed with ovarian cancer had a five-year survival rate of just 47-percent. I just got my wife back, got myself straightened out, and now faced a less than a coin flip chance that Amy would be around in five years.

Instead of freaking out, I prayed and begged God to spare her and especially Zachary this. I'm not saying I wasn't scared or wasn't doubting at moments in time, but I was learning from my past mistakes. I knew Amy needed me now more than ever and I had my second chance. I was intent not to blow it. Our church surrounded us with support and prayer, and we did what we needed to do to get through.

Upon hearing all of this, Amy's friend Cindy who was recently laid off from her job in Atlanta, put her life on hold for over a month and flew out to be with us. She was an incredible help to Amy, Zack and I, seeing us through the trial and seeing Amy through the surgery. The sacrifice she made was so incredible. Shortly after her arrival on July 31, after the sun got low and the heat got a little more tolerable, we went for a walk around the park trails near our Seven Hills home. It was here I was talking with Cindy and taking Zack for a bike ride while Amy got some rest. I expressed to her the sadness I had over possibly losing Amy. Then the prediction.

"Hold it Rich. Stop right there. I was praying with my friend back home about this and she said she received word from the Lord that this is not going to happen. Amy is not going to have cancer; she's going to survive it and she's going to be just fine. You guys are going to be just fine."

Words can't express how surreal that moment was. It was chilling but reassuring. I truly believed it. I had a peace that passed all understanding upon hearing those words. We continued in the days and weeks afterwards to pray, take time to enjoy God's creation in the Southwest, and spend time with family, friends and our church that loved us so much. The ladies at church laid hands on Amy just before her surgery with the specific prayer that she would make it through, recover, and not have cancer.

August 23rd. The surgery day arrived. It was scheduled for 1 p.m. but didn't get her in until 5 p.m. and out of surgery at 6:30 p.m. I got the news from the doctor: No cancer. It was a solid golf ball-sized mass, but it was benign. The bad news was the one ovary that had the golf ball sized mass had to be removed. We wanted to preserve it in the hopes that we could have more kids, but this was the cost of being cancer free. The prediction and prayers came true. By mid-October, Amy had fully recovered from surgery, no cancer and no back issues.

One night after the dust settled, we had dinner and an honest conversation. What now? The reality was we had put down roots in southern Nevada. Our hearts were back in central New York. We would go back if we could. If not, find somewhere like home. We left it in God's hands.

Chapter 16
Please don't let Zack die

We used to get sick often in Las Vegas. It may have been from the dust, dry air or the confines of a tightly packed metropolitan area that Las Vegas and southern Nevada is.

Zack ran high fevers of 102 all the time. On this Saturday Feb. 16th, President's Day Weekend, Mark Enjem's brother, Tony, was getting together with me for the day. Tony lived out there, and I saw him often, especially because of my long friendship with his brother. We planned to drive to Zion National Park in southern Utah. It was a perfect day trip with sunshine and mild temperatures, perfect for winter there in the Southwest.

Despite Zack waking up with a 102-degree fever and throwing up, Amy didn't want me to miss time with Tony. I needed the break and we had been through several of these episodes with Zack before which all turned out fine. We went ahead as planned. Three hours to Zion, three hours at Zion then three hours back. We would switch on my return, so Amy could go babysit for friends that night.

Tony and I arrived at Zion when Amy called my cell. She said Zack was not better and something this time was just not right. Amy wanted me to come home immediately and of course we agreed. Tony and I still enjoyed our three-hour ride back and we both thought it was just out of an abundance of caution.

Upon our return Amy shared the latest on Zack's condition and that he just received his medicine. She then went to babysit, and I was left with Zack at the house. He fell asleep. I settled in bed with him, watching Discovery Channel for about an hour. As I got up to go to the bathroom, I looked at Zack. Something was wrong.

His color was gone. I could see his pulse racing through his neck. I measured it at 180 bpm. I took his temperature. Despite getting his medicine an hour prior, his fever went from 102 degrees to over 105 degrees. I tried waking him up and he wouldn't wake up. His eyes were white, and he was limp picking him up off the bed. I got ready quickly and rushed him to the ER. I had called Amy to update her and to call her friends back for their kids, so she could join me at the hospital.

Within an hour we met back up and were in the ER. It was overcrowded, and despite his dire condition, others there were worse. Those hours late Saturday night into Sunday morning felt like forever. I prayed God would spare Zack's life and that he would make it through. We both kept praying that. It took hours before a doctor finally saw him and figured out, he had pneumonia.

It was acute and very bad. He was moved to pediatric ICU for three days, and they started intense treatment on him to bring him back to normal. What made it worse was that the all-nighter in the ER wore me down and I ended up sick with bronchitis. I couldn't even be at the hospital to comfort Zack. Amy as always was the faithful trooper by Zack's bed, loving him and not leaving him alone.

He made it. We all made it through. The "Unseen Hand of God" literally carried us through that. It was a test of faith we didn't want but made it through. Zack still has impacts from that to this day. Kids who get this tend to get walking pneumonia and he can't run long distances.

Chapter 17
40 days and 40 nights Part 1

I saw it coming before the rest of the world did. When you work in sales and marketing, you are on the front lines with small and medium size business owners. When the economy is in trouble and numbers are down, a clear majority of business owners cut spending on advertising and participation in outside promotions first. We won't go into why that's a dumb idea and why downturns are times to hold fast. There are plenty of business books I could recommend to you on that topic. But it was something I saw coming months before the panic and hysteria hit the masses in Las Vegas and the nation about the crashing economy in 2008.

I noticed it during the 2007 holiday season and in how terrible things were in the winter and spring of 2008 for businesses there. Most of them told me *"we're off 30 percent from last year"*. Where I worked those numbers started to translate into losses. Though not as steep of losses as others, when a company demands 30 percent growth per year and you are trending down 30 percent for the year 2008, that's not good. The math to pay people, make investments to grow and profit just wasn't there anymore. At some point, push was going to come to shove.

The losses continued through the summer and by September the whole nation was in panic. The stock market was in freefall. Mass layoffs were beginning around the country. Companies in southern Nevada were laying off workers in large numbers. It was like watching a line of severe thunderstorms coming in. You know it's coming and there is nothing you can do. Based on the fact we were as busy as we could be through the end of October, but there were no events or sponsorships booked beyond that as there had been in years past, I figured we'd be okay through our busy season and the axe would fall during the holidays. I had the right idea, but my timing was off.

Oct. 1 was a typical sunny day in the desert. I noticed the corporate director of human resources was walking into the building about the same time as me. It got my attention, but I wasn't thinking that was the day. We were so busy with finishing projects and sponsorship work for several clients. A huge event sponsorship I had landed for the company and took from our main competitor in town was coming up that weekend. I was in the middle of working 20 days straight, including weekends.

It was just after 9:30 a.m. when the public relations director smiled at me and said, *"Rich you need to go to the HR office."*

I knew in that instant I was done. The HR assistant rushed out to escort me into the office. Fellow co-workers looked up and realized what was starting to happen, gasped and looked at me like "Oh, no." I went through the motions and I held my head high. I spoke well of them and was not upset in any way but accepting of my fate. I will say that the act of being escorted out to my car with human resources watching me was humiliating. I understand why companies do it, so I didn't take it personally.

I was unemployed for the first time since I was 15. I had no one to work for, and no prospects. The economy was crashing. We were back to living with mom and dad, because the impending crash had forced the landlords of our Seven Hills home to kick us out as they went into foreclosure a few months prior. I went back to where my parents lived and just sat out by the pool in the sun and warmth. I didn't care that the weather was perfect. I was so down and wondering what to do next. My dad told me to forget about it and took me out to lunch with his friends then hang out in the sports book. It didn't help. I had to put my faith in God that he had us in his hands, but I had work to do.

I activated my network all around the country, looking for any job. Anywhere. I unexpectedly got some hot leads and got in the running for a few jobs in Las Vegas within days of being laid off. It was the call the day after to my old friend and general manager, Steve, back home in central New York that gave me a sense of relief. He had gone to another media in Utica as the general manager.

I asked him for help, and any job leads to come home. He said "I need two salespeople! You want to come back and work for me again?"

As I worked out whether it would be best and to give a fair shake to the leads in Las Vegas, I was given a little time. I took a few days to go up to Ely with my dad for some mountain therapy to clear my head and prepare. I went on several interviews when I came back to Las Vegas and there were several good possibilities but nothing concrete. We had to decide: Do we stay in Vegas and hope something good ultimately comes through before we run out of money? Or do we go back home to central New York, where I had a job waiting with an old friend, a return to our family there and a network of people to work with?

Amy and I went to Sonata Park in Seven Hills, to discuss and pray as we looked down on the Las Vegas Valley below. After considering the positives and negatives, walking, talking and most importantly giving much prayer to God for direction, we were not at peace staying in southern Nevada anymore. We decided to return home to central New York.

It took ten days to settle affairs in Las Vegas, pull up stakes, and get a trailer hitched to our minivan. It was time to get the rental trailer to haul our stuff back and start packing fast! I put Amy, Zack and our dog, Rolly, in the Santa Fe with the car top carrier. I drove the (probably overloaded) minivan. It was jam packed with not even a square inch to spare! After tearful goodbyes with our friends, our close family friend Ellen (who was like a grandma to Zack) and my mom and dad, we left on the afternoon of Oct. 26th for good.

Between the packing and adventure driving across country back home, you'd think it was a great time. It was by far the most stressful cross country drive I've ever done. I've had a little experience with a trailer, but nothing like this. It was hard work and we didn't have the luxury of switching off drivers if we got tired. If we were tired, we both stopped for as long as we had to.

Less than a hundred miles into the trip we noticed a slow leak in one of the trailer tires. This had me freaked out as tire blowouts were very common in the Southwest with the dry climate and high speeds. A tire blowout on the trailer would have meant losing all our stuff, and probably me with it! There is no way a minivan at maximum capacity towing a trailer would be able to maintain control in a tire blowout. Going off the road and/or flipping over in a spectacular crash would have been the likely result. Thankfully that did not happen.

We continued onward and upward. It became clear every time we hit a hill we would slow down. Despite having a V6 engine, the minivan was not happy. We were running 12 miles per gallon, with no power on the hills. The flashers were on a lot. And the "hills" coming up the Virgin River Gorge to St. George and Cedar City, Utah were nothing compared to the Wasatch Range, the Rockies and the Continental Divide ahead.

After an overnight at a roadside motel in central Utah, we tried the next day to make it to our friend Jay's in Cheyenne, Wyo. I thought we'd never make it. We were 8 hours away when we started but it took over 13 hours to get there. We had to climb from Provo to Park City to get to I-80. The climb was so long and so high, we were reduced to less than 20 mph on the highway. It was dangerous and scary, but we made it. We crossed the divide before dark and made it over the last mountain between Laramie and Cheyenne without incident.

I was so happy to have the Rockies behind me, good friends in front of me as hosts, comfortable beds and an amazing breakfast the next morning.

The Great Plains were much nicer to us in terms of driving and stress on the minivan. Two days later we made it to Chicago. We were wearing down. We made one last big push before dawn to get from Chicago to Syracuse, N.Y. on Oct. 30th. We made it! Larry and Suzann welcomed us in a tear-filled reunion and a hearty "welcome home" celebration. Just 64 miles were left on Halloween 2008.

After 2,600 miles of white-knuckle driving, we were now where we never thought we'd see. Home not just to visit but to stay. We pulled into Mamwah's driveway, Amy's childhood home, in Barneveld. She and Amy's sister Bonnie came running out to hug us and shed some tears. We were away exactly 3 ½ years in southern Nevada, but central New York was always "home". We took home for granted before.

We moved in temporarily with friends in Poland and began reuniting with many who missed us the previous 3 ½ years and start to rebuild our life again in central New York. It was a sweet time of many reunions, hugs and celebrations.

On Nov. 10th, 40 days and nights since the layoff, I returned to work. I was so fortunate, especially since the economy was in shambles at the time.

Out of the 40 Days and 40 Nights began another great run of several years with my old general manager Steve on the sales side of the media business. There I grew tremendously under him and the great team to be around. Without what I went through in Las Vegas, the homecoming and success afterwards would have never happened.

Chapter 18
The prayer for more children

Amy's ovarian cancer scare and the surgery that took out one of her ovaries, made bearing children again a long shot. We tried for a few years and did use some therapies to help things along, but nothing worked. We were not kids anymore. Amy and I had already passed 35 with 40 just ahead. Zachary had just turned 8. It was now the summer of 2011. Economically, we were still struggling to recover from the crash of 2008 and the recession of 2009, as most still were at the time. Our window for having more children was growing smaller. As sad as we were at the time that Zack could be it for children, we had to accept that could be God's plan for our lives.

We had gone with several friends from our church to the dedication of a large ministry center in the Adirondack Mountains outside Piseco, NY run by Adirondack Bible Chapel. We knew many of the people there and had become friends with a few of them. This ministry center was a six-year labor of love. They restored an old Adirondack Camp on 250 acres, as a place for people from around the world who need help or counseling, a retreat from life and a place for spiritual growth.

July 31, 2011 was a huge celebration with hundreds attending. They had a pig roast, tours, plenty of food and fellowship. One of the ABC members got into a long conversation with my wife. Next thing I know we are hanging out and the topic came up about us wanting to have more kids. The members were Judy and her (now late) husband, Richard, who lived on nearby Lake Pleasant. Judy was moved and overcome by our story; she had such a deep burden to pray for us having more children. We pulled aside from the crowd and we all prayed together over this. It was an incredible prayer. Judy and Richard were so passionate and heartfelt with the prayers lifted to God. If they had any power to make a baby appear, they would have. We were invited back to their home on Lake Pleasant for an awesome dinner then brought to Camp of the Woods for Sunday night worship and prayer. That was an incredible experience. The new friends we made, and their heartfelt prayers were moving.

I wasn't sure Amy would be able to have more kids, even after those incredible prayers. But the prayers were specifically that we would be able to "have" more children. I never keyed into that until much later, but for us to be able to "have" more children was the prayer. That, somehow and some way I did believe all along. We just knew from family and friends that have done private adoption domestically and overseas that it is prohibitively expensive. I know there are many people that do great work with private adoptions, but I can't understand why they must drag the process out so long, and charge tens of thousands of dollars. We didn't have that kind of money.

But we had to believe the prayer. At some point, God would answer. Philippians 4:6-7 ESV *"Do not be anxious about anything, <u>but in everything by prayer and supplication with thanksgiving let your requests be made known to God</u>. And the peace of God, which surpasses all understanding, will guard your hearts and minds in Christ Jesus."*

That was where we rested our faith as best as we could. The months went on after this day, and, still, nothing. It took almost 18 months afterwards before we were made aware of adoptions happening through foster care locally. We then became aware of the great need in our area for adoptive and foster families. Not knowing where the path would lead, or even realizing at the time this was God's answer to our prayer, we started the process to become foster parents locally.

The paperwork, background checks, and process is intense. You then need 40 hours of training, which we did in 13 weeks of classes from February to May 2013. It was honestly just like going back to college. The coursework was very informative and very intensive. The interview process more thorough than any job you'll ever have. They inspect your home, your water well, smoke detectors, fire extinguishers, beds, safety issues, anything you could think of!

It may sound overwhelming, and it can be. It can seem overbearing but it's necessary because there are kids lives involved here. It may sound like it's not worth all the trouble. Trust me, in the end, with perseverance; the rewards far outweigh the trouble you must go through. Is it a sacrifice? Yes! But nothing worthwhile is easy.

We worked hard in attending and passing the classes, inspections and making sure all our paperwork was in order. In May 2013 we were formally certified as foster parents, ready to take in children. We knew there was a great need out there. We also knew that there was no idea what could come up, when, and under what circumstances. You have no control over that. Foster care needs you to be willing and ready. We were.

All we were waiting for was the phone call.

Chapter 19
Emergency respite

It was July 24, 2013. An unusually chilly and cloudy summer afternoon. Amy was home with Zack while I was out working for a client. Her phone rang. It was the foster care agency. They said they had an "emergency respite" and wanted to know if we could take in a 13-month-old girl temporarily. Amy said yes. Fifteen minutes later, Ariella came to our home for the first time.

Amy called me to get home ASAP, and I did. We had everything ready for a young child or baby, but we were starting blind. I can't imagine how scary it was for Ariella. Even though she had no way of comprehending it like we can as adults I'm sure, somehow, she knew.

That first night was rough and long. We did the best we could to love and comfort her. Ariella was dirty; she had been neglected and abandoned for an unknown period, presumably for a few days, and had major rashes on her body.

The next morning, we had to bring her down to the foster care agency so the nurse could check her and for us to discuss next steps. Amy and I asked the question: So, who is going to take her now? The nurse said "Well we need to find a longer-term foster home for her. Would you guys be willing to foster Ariella?"

We instantly said, "Yes!"

This was the start of many restless nights, countless doctors' appointments, monthly meetings with case workers and the ups and downs of being a foster parent. There is no way around it, being on an emotional roller coaster. You must love and take care of the children, as if they are your own, yet they are not. That is what they need the most from any foster family, that love, acceptance and stability that you can provide. If they are placed in the foster care system, it's because they were in a very bad situation. It can be a hard adjustment for all. It's not for the faint of heart. There is a great need for foster families that is only growing month after month, year after year.

In most cases, the birth parents and/or their extended families are involved. As much as you try to work with them to help them, as a neutral party, they can look at you as the enemy. These families that have lost their children and gone through trauma themselves. They also know that if they do not follow orders from the court and from authorities, you could end up with their child permanently. It makes for awkward situations.

Sometimes children in foster care come to you for just a few weeks, but it can be for several months or even years. They could stay with you permanently. Every foster care case is different with its own unique circumstances.

In any foster care situation, it's possible the children could leave your home and return to the birth parents or their family, even if you are in the process of adopting them. It is so hard to give that love to someone that may leave you and you have no control over the situation. You don't want to be hurt. I get it. Amy and I felt the same way, too. Love is a wonderful thing to have and to get, and a terribly painful thing to lose.

We heard so often back then, and still today, this sentiment: *"Oh I couldn't do that. I just couldn't love them and then possibly have to let them go. It would be too hard. It would break our hearts and it would be so hard to live with the pain."*

This reaction is normal. My wife and I had it, too. People in general don't want to intentionally put themselves in a position where they could be hurt. But may I submit to you some other thoughts for consideration. What if we stay there in that place, believing those words, and as a result of the fear of getting hurt alone, we don't try at all? Is this a sinful and selfish reaction? Are we contradicting ourselves?

If you have children of your own right now, did you ever consider not having one because they could get killed in an accident, kidnapped, or they could get very sick and die? The divorce rate in this country is around 50-percent, but did that stop you from seeking after your soulmate? Did it stop you from marrying them? Though most relationships don't last a lifetime anymore, like previous generations, you still try, right?

The fear of our loss should not be preventing so many from reaching out and giving love to children that so desperately need it. Even if it's only for a short time, or for a longer time with a chance of adopting and having it fall through in the end.

It's not about our needs. It's about theirs. It's not about what we get but what we give.

Why am I saying this? We experienced the whole wide range of emotions with Ariella on our two-and-a-half year, 800+ day journey from foster care to adoption. We came very close to losing her, on more than one occasion, because of the changing situations with her birth family. We lived this. We have no regrets. And it was all worth it. It's easy to say because this story had a happily ever after in it. Yes, we were prepared to accept along the way if it wasn't. It would have been hard, but we would have made it through.

Chapter 20
Can't utter the word "no"

It was a perfect sunny and warm July afternoon, July 11, 2014. Even more perfect because it was a Friday! I had been away all day with my boss Mike for appointments with clients in Albany. We had just completed the drive back to the Canastota exit of the Thruway, minutes from the home we just moved to there, and where Mike's car was. It was 3:45 p.m.

The moment I said goodbye to Mike, my phone rang. It was Amy. She sounded a little off.

"Rich," she said, "I just got a call for newborn twins. They're at Crouse in Syracuse, six weeks premature, one is being released and they have no place to go."

I had started the new job under Mike a few months prior. We had moved to Canastota, a beautiful town where many people split their commutes between Syracuse and Utica. We had our hands full with Ariella. My mom was living with us. Life was crazy and barely manageable. From a logical perspective, there was no way we would take a set of *twins* into your home under those circumstances. The thought was crazy and terrifying. How could we do it?

My friends, that's not how God works. Things are never nice and neatly packaged for our convenience. Many times, blessings are given to you as challenges. Sometimes you are presented with what seems impossible, so God can work through us and everyone around us.

After Amy explained the situation, I wanted so bad to say no, and I physically tried to. But I couldn't say the word "No." It was one of the freakiest things ever. I could talk but though I tried to say no, my voice physically could not. If that's not the "Unseen Hand of God" working, I don't know what is.

When I realized I couldn't speak, "No," I said *"honey, can you call them back and find out any more information? And you're ok doing this? You're the expert with babies and I'm working 60 hours a week. I'll do the best I can, but you are the one spending the most time with them"*. I ended our conversation with this: *"Whatever God puts on your heart honey, go with it. I trust you."*

Amy called right back and asked if they had found a home yet for the twins. They had not. She got a little more information and had thought about saying "No" herself, but she physically couldn't say it either. She wanted to take them in and knew she could do it having cared for multiples before in prior babysitting jobs. But Amy was scared it might be too much and didn't want to make things too hard on me, Zack, Ariella or my mom. She prayed quickly, took a deep breath, and said *"Ok we'll do it!"*

Two hours later, Lillian arrived at our home. Her twin, Aiden, was only three pounds and was still at the hospital. She was four pounds. Her legs were the size of my finger. Her arms were even smaller. I could hold her in the palm of my hand. It was the tiniest, most fragile baby, I had ever seen in person. I was so scared I didn't want to be around Amy and Lillian at all for fear of accidentally hurting her. I vigorously helped her in any other way I could and let her take care of the tiny baby. 24 hours after taking her in, Amy said, "Aren't you going to hold her?"

I did, and I lost it. I was so scared I would hurt her. I was so overwhelmed by my fears that I couldn't say no.

"Honey, I can't do this," I said. "I think it's too much for me, too much for us."

Amy loves babies so much that I feared this might upset her, but it didn't.

"You're probably right," she surprised me by replying. "But let's pray on it and head to church in the morning. We have her until at least Monday anyway."

Despite our new home being 45 minutes away from our home church, we kept making the drive each Sunday. They were our friends, and many were like family to us. This day was the brightest shining example of that. They knew we just took in the first twin and were waiting on the second to come home to us and unbeknownst to us, had already sprang into action. Upon arriving at church, we were overwhelmed with diapers, preemie clothes and all kinds of things we'd need that now we didn't have to buy. It was amazing. Despite this outpouring of love and seeing the "Unseen Hand of God" moving right before my eyes, I still had my mind set we'd ask them to find another family the next day. I still had the fear I couldn't do it.

We went to the nursery and listened to the service through the speakers. In the nursery were my mentor and long-time trusted friend Tom and his wife Karen. Tom loved holding babies. He was also one of the leaders of the church. Tom was a strong man of God, an electrician with a successful business, a humble servant to his wife and five kids. He also was ready and willing to help anyone in need. Tom was "the man".

At this point, he hadn't heard about the twins yet, so we brought him up to speed. He said, "God just added two more kids to your family. They're yours. You've been so blessed brother." I'm like "Tom, they're just foster, we don't know the situation yet, and I think we're going to see if they can find another home for them. I think it may be too much for us now."

"They're yours!" Tom stopped me immediately and said emphatically with a big smile, "They don't need another home; they have your home! They aren't going to leave you."

Within moments, Tom and Karen spoke through us with amazing words of encouragement, love and power from God. By the time service was over, it was a done deal. We would keep them, foster them, and leave it in God's hands for their future.

I was about to turn away one of the greatest gifts of my life, without ever meeting Aiden. He was all alone at the hospital. There was no one to hold him and care for him like a mom, just the dedicated NICU nurses. And by the way they aren't just nurses. Those in the NICU are literally angels, providing specialized and critical care to ensure babies not only survive but thrive. Their training and compassion save the lives of so many babies who might not make it without their care. And that's exactly what they were doing for Aiden.

We met Aiden the next day, Monday the 14th, and got to hold the three-pound wonder. Even smaller than Lillian, fighting to stay alive as his body temperature kept dropping without the isolet. We had to be specially taught how to feed him and hold him because of his size and fragility. After holding him for the first time I promised this tiny boy that I would take him home and he could stay with us as long as he could; forever if we could. Every night that week, after leaving work in downtown Syracuse at 5 p.m. I'd visit the NICU, feed Aiden and hold him. We made sure that we were there to feed him, hold him and love him until he was released. We prayed it would be soon.

That next Monday he was released. Amy got to do something she always wanted to do: Bring home a newborn baby left alone at the hospital to raise and love. It meant the world to her, because not being able to have more kids anymore, this was the only other way for it to happen.

Lillian and Aiden, "the twins," as we called them, had a long journey ahead of them. They had to stay healthy, gain weight, have a special diet and go to many doctor visits. It was as hard as I feared it would be, but something was happening to all of us. God was growing us in ways which we could never have dreamed. Hearts were changing, dreams were changing, and our lives were changing, all for the better.

Was it easy? No. Was it worth it? I can't imagine my life without those kids. I can't imagine our family without those kids. Without "the twins" our family just isn't our family. The experience of caring for preemie twins, one with significant medical problems and complications, is not for everyone. We had to give up so much of our life at the time, but we received so much more than we could have ever dreamed.

I'm so glad God kept Amy and me from uttering "no". I believe God gave Tom the right words and encouragement for me that fateful Sunday. I am thankful that we never gave up on each other through many sleepless nights, health scares and crazy trials. I am so thankful to God for how He has blessed us with both patience and power.

You can do far more than you think you can when you go to your source of strength and hope, God's only son, Jesus Christ. You can't change the world, but you can change the world for the people around you. To those people you will mean the world to them.

Chapter 21
Adoption

The adoption process through foster care is a long journey. It takes several months to a few years to complete. If children remain technically in foster care, there is always that chance a distant family member could pop up out of nowhere and lay claim to the child. It happens more often than you think. You never have the assurance, even if you've done everything right and asked of you, that you will ultimately adopt the child. Even if you are well into the formal process of adoption, until it is signed by a judge and formally decreed by the court, you must be guarded in your heart.

This is probably one of the reasons why adoption is so special. It takes so much to get there and it's a permanent, lifelong commitment. In many ways it's like a marriage, but it's more binding than that. After adoption, you can't give up on the kid, no matter how tough the going gets. In foster care, you always have the ten-day notice to get out. After adoption, they are yours, as if they were born to you, legally and otherwise. No turning back. You are all in.

As I wrote earlier, Ariella had been with us for two and a half years before her adoption was complete. From the beginning, we loved her as our own. Ariella went from not walking, talking, or crawling, with no hair, at 13 months, to a bright smile; a spring in her step and a fierce spirit of life awakened in her. We witnessed a miracle from a child that was brought to us from a bad situation and blossomed to life like a flower in the spring.

It was National Adoption Day. This special day is always the Friday prior to Thanksgiving. Around the country, many adoptions happen on this day. In central New York, it's at the

OnCenter in Syracuse. Hundreds cram into the convention center for a special ceremony presided by judges from across the region and several dignitaries. It's a happy day with balloons and gifts all over the place for adoptive families. If you have never been to one, I highly recommend you go to one.

This is the day we signed on the dotted line. The judge decreed that Ariella is forever a Lupia! Right after that the "bell" rang, signaling the adoption was 100-percent complete. A new life with the new family began! The emotion of that moment and the celebration for days afterwards right into Thanksgiving, is something I wish everyone could experience.

As I mentioned before, it's like a wedding, but different. It's like the actual birth of a child, but different. I just remember feeling so full of joy like I had rarely felt in my life. We couldn't help to think back to Judy's prayer in 2011, or our first thoughts and talks of adoption in Las Vegas as early as 2005. We were now officially one boy and one girl, the two that we always wanted to have, but the twins were with us, and it was looking likely that their turn could come next.

We asked for a blessing, a miracle, and God delivered beyond our wildest dreams in a way only He could do. We are so incredibly blessed by Ariella. It was our privilege to adopt her! We are so incredibly blessed that her "forever family" as it was called, is with us.

If you stop and think about it, isn't our relationship with God like an adoption? It is. It's actually in the Bible, in Ephesians 1:3-10 ESV *"Blessed be the God and Father of our Lord Jesus Christ, who has blessed us in Christ with every spiritual blessing in the heavenly places even as he chose us in him before the foundation of the world, that we should be holy and blameless before him. <u>In love He predestined us for adoption to himself as sons through Jesus Christ</u>, according to the purpose of his will, to the praise of his glorious grace, with which he has blessed us in the Beloved. In him we have redemption through his blood, the forgiveness of our* *trespasses, according to the riches of his grace which he lavished upon us, in all wisdom and insight making known] to us the mystery of his will, according to his purpose, which he set forth in Christ as a plan for the fullness of time, to unite all things in him, things in heaven and things on earth.*

We are ALL adopted! You were adopted as a child of God through Jesus Christ. I was adopted!

The God of this universe wants to be with you, and have you experience the amazing grace, forgiveness of our trespasses and to be with him. Despite all you've done to mess things up, like me, despite times you've acted selfishly, like me, and despite times you have not believed, walked away and/or doubted, especially like me…

You are loved by God. You are his child. He wants to adopt you right now.

The question is, are you willing to be his child? He wants everyone to come but knows not everyone will.
Therefore, He said, "Chose us in Him" in verse four. If you are a child of God, like me, you need to be constantly reminded of His love and His promises for us. If you are not, if you are alone and can't do it on your own anymore and are tired of fighting the battles God already won for you, then cry out to Him. Pray to Him. Ask Him to forgive you of your sins, come into your life, change you, and bring people into your life to help you along (fellowship) through life.

If you are a child of God and have messed up, even walked away, it's just like a legal adoption contract for a child. It's forever. It's irrevocable. You know in your heart what you need to do. You need to confess whatever you've done, repent (change the ways that got you into trouble) and ask for God to restore you. He will. You've seen this in my story already. You must believe his will for you. If it's not true, then why is the Prodigal Son in the Bible in Luke Chapter 15?

That's why God laid it on my heart to write this in the first place. I want to encourage you to the way, the truth and the life, and to experience firsthand your adoption by God through Jesus Christ, or to come home like a prodigal to where you belong and begin again.

The "Unseen Hand of God" is on your heart right now if you've read this far. What are you going to do? We all have mountains to climb and I know who is carrying me.

Chapter 22
Mount Marcy

Mount Marcy was the one I always wanted to hike since I was a kid. It's the big one if you are a New York State native. While there are 46 peaks 4,000 feet or higher, it's the only one that's over a mile high. It's a long hike but nowhere near as hard of a vertical ascent as other peaks. People like me could do it. But I always made excuses. I didn't want to do it alone. The weather had to be good. I didn't know where to go or whom to ask. It was on my bucket list and at 40 you realize you don't have forever. Are you going to do it? Yes. I had a lot more weight on me than I wanted and was not in the best shape, but I knew a good attitude, preparation and encouragement would make the difference.

Quarter to three in the morning was a time I was familiar with when I got up and ready to deliver the morning weather on TV. Even when you are excited to get up, it's rough. I double-checked everything, woke Zack up, got him in the car, kissed Amy goodbye and set out on our trip. Over three hours driving to the trailhead at the Loj, an all-day hike, and the long drive back at night.

I needed to be ready mentally and awake enough to drive through the Adirondack wilderness in the dark to start, then later at dawn, a popular time for two big problems, fog and deer.

Not even one mile into the trip, I nearly hit a deer crossing Trenton Road and had to screech to a stop. As frustrated as I was at that happening, the thought came to me immediately: Things happen for a reason. Just accept it and go on. I took a deep breath, then got us on the highway, over

Deerfield Hill and out towards the black wilderness ahead. Over three hours to go still.

We had all day to do the hike and we could stay up there the night if we had to, but we had to be at Marcy Dam at 7 a.m. to meet Suzann and her friends, who camped there the night before. I knew we weren't going to make it 2.5 miles from the Adirondack Loj to Marcy Dam by 7 a.m. We set out from the Loj register at 6:40 a.m. and Zack and I took a steady pace. The last thing I wanted was to reach the summit 7.6 miles and 3,165 vertical feet ahead of me too late in the afternoon and needing to use the headlamps on the way out. The trail from Loj to Marcy Dam is a little up, a little down, but otherwise a beautiful walk in the woods. We finally reached the dam at 7:35 a.m. and met up with Suzann and our party. We snapped some pictures and chatted for a little while, preparing for the hike ahead. Suzann predicted we would reach the summit at 1 p.m.

We crossed the dam bridge and reached the T with the trail from South Meadows, another parking area near the Loj, at 7:55 a.m. Then, the God moment happened.

Pete, our church deacon, and ADK 46er (one who has climbed all 46 high peaks), was with his hiking "peeps" on their way to hike Mt. Colden via the popular "trap dike". The trails intersect at Marcy Dam, combine for a few hundred yards then split off again. We didn't plan to meet. We were all surprised and very happy to see each other. We hugged, snapped a few pictures, then he had to catch back up to his party.

"It's easy Rich," Pete said, on the way out. "Piece of cake. You got this."

As he faded into the woods, and we continued up our trail, I was completely overcome by tears and joy. I knew God's hand was on the day, and that I was going to make it. No matter what I was going to make it! The feeling was indescribable and not something you can recreate.

We made great time and were ahead of pace most of the morning. Clouds developed over the mountain as temperatures rose and gave cover to the blazing sun. The climb was steady and sure, but not steep or intimidating at all. In three hours, we were already over 4,000 feet and approaching the Great Range trail intersection when we came to "the meadow" as I called it and got my first glimpse of the summit. I was slowly wearing down and feeling the fact we already walked six miles and climbed 2,300 vertical feet, more than twice the height of the Empire State Building. I confirmed on GPS we were just over 4,500 feet and what I saw in front of me, the "ants' climbing the summit rising yet another 800 feet vertical.

I should have taken a picture, but I didn't. I was weary. I knew I'd make the last 1.6 miles; I just didn't know how long. It was 11:45 a.m. and I needed to stop more frequently as we approached the tree line. I just kept saying *"One foot in front of the other"*, and sometimes painfully so. I was holding up our party. I made it clear, *please don't leave me alone.* But they did for a while. That was the hardest part. Then Zack came back for me. He was scared that I would have a heart attack or vomit or something. I just asked him to help me the last bit to the top. The grade started to level off on the rocks, the amazing view was all around me, and we were into the winds that are almost constant at the summit. I took my last steps with Zack and set foot on the summit at exactly 1 p.m., just as Suzann said.

Victory. I broke down. I accomplished a lifelong dream.

After five minutes I gained my composure and took in the astonishing scene around me. The pictures and video became permanently seared into my mind of God's creation, what I did to get there and the reward for not giving up. It's the only place I've been east of the Mississippi that reminds me of being west of the Mississippi, up in the Rockies and the Intermountain West, of the scraggly rocks of Little Haystack and Haystack. The rounded bald domes like Mt. Skylight and the intimidating Great Range, including Gothics, as scary looking as it sounds. There was also the stunning, volcano cone shape of Mt. Colden.

Looking around and knowing what it takes to reach these mountains gave me so much respect for the 46ers. This made the accomplishment of climbing one of them, the biggest one, that much more special. It was an honor and a privilege to have one hour on the rooftop of New York. It was a great challenge taken and conquered. Of all the best memories of my life, this day no doubt is near the top.

That hour seemed to fly by. It was way too short for the work put in. But we had 7.6 miles to go, and downhill for a big guy like me is not necessarily easy. Gravity plus too much weight on the knees equals OUCH! Thankfully the easier grade meant I made better time down the mountain, but it still seemed like forever. One place we passed on the way up but stopped on the way back was Indian Falls. It features a stunning view of the Macintyre Range (Wright Mt., Algonquin Mt. and Iroquois Mt.) Nestled around 3,500 feet, its three miles and about 1,800 feet vertical below the summit. It's an incredible halfway point, and if you run low on water and have a filter, it's a perfect spot to fill up with water. The water is so cold it feels like it's from your refrigerator! We took over a half hour to rest on the rocks in the sun, soak our feet in the ice-cold water, and reflect on the great day.

We moved quickly down the rest of the mountain and made it back to Marcy Dam at 6:15 p.m. Zack and I said goodbye to our crew. We set off to hike to the Loj parking lot 2.5 miles ahead. I figured we could make it fast. While it's somewhat flat, you don't notice the bumps and slight ups and downs when you're fresh. You hit any up or down on a hiking trail after 12 miles on a mountain, it becomes painful! That last stretch was almost as hard as the last steps up Marcy quite honestly. I felt like I was starting to "bonk" (or have my body involuntarily shut down to where I couldn't walk any further) about halfway between the dam and the Loj.

I reached into my pack and downed a handful of raisins, took the last bit of water I had and tried to breathe easy. It worked. I was scared in the still of the wilderness with sweet food in my mouth knowing bears could come around quickly. Thankfully, we never saw one. At 7:15 p.m. we reached the parking lot. It was time to change and get out of dodge! After phoning home to let Amy know we made it back safely and were driving home, we stopped quickly for pictures then a celebratory snack stop at Stewarts in Keene.

Don't try to do what we did in one day. As expensive and tough to get accommodations are on a weekend in the Adirondacks, especially on demand in summer, it's well worth it. After passing Schroon Lake, I started to feel my body shut down from the intense hike. I still had two hours in the dark to get home from there. Most of the remaining drive was through wilderness with no cell coverage, with many miles between towns. I believe by grace and the "Unseen Hand of God" we got through it and reached cell signal at 11:15 p.m. I called Amy and asked her to stay on the phone until we pulled into the house. At 11:30, 20+ hours after we left, we were home safe in our beds.

There are so many reasons why this ranks high on the list of the best days of my life. Perseverance and running the race in such a way to receive the prize always has a reward. When you are forced to dig down deep to get through something bad or to get to something good, God will give you what you need to make it. If you let Him. One of the biggest things I've had to overcome in life has been, well, me. I've been short circuited by my own doubts and lack of faith. I'm sure we've all been there at one time or another. If you are there more often than others, it doesn't matter. Tomorrow is a new day. You can do it! I can and I will! Changing your perspective to a positive one, letting God work through you, can make all the difference. I didn't let labels or doubts stop me from an incredible mountaintop experience. You shouldn't either.

Chapter 23
Celebration!

Ariella's adoption day was so nice, we decided to do it again! The long and winding road with Lillian and Aiden after two years of foster care was finally about to end in adoption. Everything was resolved, and the process was started in the summer of 2016 with enough time to get everything done in time for National Adoption Day. The people I worked with in Syracuse were so moved by our story with Ariella and the twins, they wanted to be there, but it was during the workday. My boss, Mike, couldn't make it because of an important meeting the prior year but made sure he could come this time.

What he didn't tell me was what he planned with my teammates. There were nine of us total on the team including myself and Mike, Rob, Patti, Brandon, JP, James, Will and Jeff. I was in the OnCenter with my family expecting just Mike to come find me… but they all came! I knew they all had work to do, but Mike encouraged them to put things aside and make the short trek across downtown to see the adoptions. They all came willingly. What an amazing sight that was to see everyone on the team walking up to us all with big smiles on their faces, hugs and high fives!

Very few people in this world will ever get to experience what I did in those moments. To see the full support of not just my family, but my boss and our entire team at work, still leaves me in shock to this day. Work is important, business is important, profits are important. No sane businessperson will ever argue this. What has, unfortunately, been debated is the importance of people. Many corporations look at positions like a cog in a wheel and not people. When you invest in people, build them up and put others first, amazing things happen. Things like this have great impact!

We had the largest crowd around our table with the twins, our family, friends from work, and the judge; over 30 people! As with the previous adoption, and just like with any legal business, the judge explains to you and to everyone clearly what is being signed, why, and the long-term implications of your decision. The judge even had to go through our applications and asked me to verify who my employer was. I got to smile, and say, "They are right here with us."

"Wow!" the judge exclaimed, followed by a hearty cheer from our team!

When the judge concluded the paperwork, she rang the bell for both adoptions and a bigger cheer was let out. After receiving the final paperwork moments later, the judge gave a bell to both Aiden and Lillian. With huge smiles on their faces, they rang them and the biggest cheer of all erupted! It felt like a victory lap after a race.

The process of fostering and adopting the twins would not have been possible without help from so many. It took a great wife at home to lovingly take care of them, a great family to encourage us, a supportive church and good friends to support you with prayer and tangible blessings when you needed them.

Add to this a great workplace that provided the flexibility to take care of family business when I needed to; they're a family that I don't deserve. God put so many great people in my way and I could never say thank you enough to those that invested so much into us.

Chapter 24
Goodbye Tom

He was the rock of his family, the church we were a part of for over a decade, and to so many others. I don't understand why God allows things to happen the way they do sometimes. If it were up to me, Tom would have been the last person I'd have taken from this Earth. But God is God, and I'm not. I need to trust Him in things I don't understand and can't see. It's a walk of faith we're good at talking about but is not easy to walk when you miss someone so much.

Tom was a mentor for many years to me. He always found the time, at just the right time, to let me talk, give me wisdom, and pray with me. When I needed help, he was there. When I was struggling in my walk with God, in my marriage, financially, with starting my own business, Tom was always there. We enjoyed a love of snowmobiling and always tried to go out for a ride at least once a winter.

A man's man, who kept his priorities straight, Tom put God first, followed by his wife, his kids and then everything else. He made others, including me, feel like part of his family.

He loved people. He invested in them, and loved those who were hard to love, like me! Tom led by example how to live by serving his wife and kids. He gave unselfishly of his time, work and money to help others. His wisdom was incredible, and boy did I need a lot of it! I still do. Tom gave the greatest big bear hugs that would take your breath away! He loved to hold babies, comfort children and correct lovingly.

He had just turned 60 and was so proud of me for finally taking his advice to buy a house instead of rent. He redid the electric service in our new home and installed new outlets in our basement that we finished. It turned out to be one of the last residential electrical jobs he ever did.

In the fall of 2016, he started getting sick and was out of work. The next thing we knew, Tom had cancer. We all prayed God would take the cancer away and that he would be restored. He went to Boston for weeks of treatment. We prayed. We hoped. But this cancer would not give up. The chemo didn't work anymore. As the winter of 2017 dragged on, hope of recovery was lost. All who knew and loved Tom prepared to say goodbye.

Tom could only have limited visits at home. We were fortunate to have a few minutes to say goodbye to him on March 27, 2017. Despite the fact he was dying, his spirits were up. He was so happy to see us and invited us into the living room so we could talk and fellowship just like old times.

He asked about our family and reminded us about how proud he was for following through from that day in 2014 he told us the twins would be ours (at that meeting, they officially were). He praised me with words of admonition for how well I was doing as a father and a husband. He was proud of me and told me to just keep working hard. Keep doing what you're doing, he said. Stay faithful to the Lord and the things you know you need to do. Love is spelled TIME. It's hard but your kids need it. He told Amy about how proud he was of how she turned out since he met her as a 12-year-old girl. Tom knew she needed someone in her life like a dad to her because her real dad had died when she was very young. He wanted so bad to see "the critters" as he jokingly called our little kids and hug them, but his condition prohibited that. And then he prayed for us and gave thanks for the miracle he performed in creating our family among so many other blessings.

My dying friend and mentor spoke life over me and my family. He never complained about his condition or fate. His heart was filled with thankfulness, unselfish actions and reckless love. What an example of faithfulness to God and everything that is right and good that he left for me and my family. A few days later, God called him home.

Why, God? Why take such a loving and faithful man, husband, father, businessman, friend and mentor to so many besides me? He could have lived so many more years and be with us today. He had so much more love to give! I can't answer that for certain and no one can. One day I'm sure I'll know.

Tom knew he was nothing without Christ. We'd say to each other, both as a joke and to humble each other, "You're nothing." A lot of times it would be over a bear hug or a tackle when you're about to be crushed into a corner. But Tom knew the truth. He knew all his love and unselfishness came from God through Jesus Christ and the Holy Spirit. It was nothing of him and all of God.

It's nothing we've done to deserve it, but by grace we are saved, lest any man should boast (Ephesians 2:8-9). We are God's children. He adopted us. And therefore, we have a father in heaven. As such we all answer ultimately to him.

My own kids sometimes don't understand why it's time to stop playing and go to bed or do something else. It doesn't seem right to them. It doesn't seem fair. They are hurt and cry initially. But I am the father of my kids and I know what they need. After they calm down, they say, "I love you, dad;" they believe it, and trust me with a childlike faith. I try to deal with grief and loss through these eyes. For me, it works. Everyone grieves differently and in their own time. Don't ever force.

We don't understand when things happen that are unpleasant and downright hurtful to us. But if I love and trust God like the father that he is, why should I approach God the same way that my own children approach me? Luke 18:17 ESV says, *"Truly I tell you, anyone who will not receive the kingdom of God like a little child will never enter it."* God, our heavenly father, knows what we need. I must have faith and trust him even though it hurts not having loved ones like him around. God is sovereign, and His will is perfect.

I'm trying every day to draw closer to God through examples like Tom, look for ways to help others, love others and encourage others like he did. He passed on a great legacy to his wife, kids and community. We all could do the same and follow the Godly example he set for us.

With grateful appreciation to Tom's family for their blessing in sharing this chapter of the book with you.

Chapter 25
Brain tumor

It started out like most summer Fridays in upstate New York, sunny and warm. It was a busy day with the push to get everything done quickly because clients vanish after lunch to get a start to the weekend.

I had an appointment at the end of the day to formally agree on a new and better offer for me to return to work in Utica. The day was bright, the future was bright, and I was upbeat. I walked into my doctor's office for my 10 a.m. follow up to check on my latest test results. It was supposed to be a quick in and out like always, and I'd be on my way.

I was brought back to the exam room immediately then left alone. The minutes dragged on. I knew quickly something was up, as they didn't come in right away. They always do, especially in the morning. Ten minutes turned to twenty and twenty-five. By this point, I was getting agitated. I started going over my appointments and stops for the day in my head and figuring what I could and couldn't do with less time. In the last moments before the door opened, I was thinking of stepping outside to ask if they forgot me.

It was 10:30 a.m. The door opened. It was Alyssa, one of the doc's nurse practitioners. She had a very long look on her face. I didn't notice that immediately, so I said enthusiastically, "Good morning! How are you?"

Alyssa paused for a moment then looked me in the eye and came right out with it as best as she could, visibly concerned.

"We think you have a brain tumor."
I was numb and stunned.

I heard everything she said afterwards about getting an MRI right away, scheduling follow up, and what kind of tumor they thought it was, but I went on autopilot. My thoughts turned inward.

The next hours were filled with frantic phone calls, moving my schedule around, contacting family and friends, trying to figure out what to do next. I got the MRI scheduled as soon as I could, the following Thursday.

At 2 p.m. the following Friday, I got the call and confirmation. It indeed was a brain tumor, a pituitary tumor, called a Prolactinoma. It was big, squishing my pituitary gland, pressing on my optic nerve and encasing a carotid artery. This alone, not counting the side effects of the tumor and hormones being way off, could have caused sudden vision loss or a stroke.

I had to be reminded, as I was that next Sunday, God is in charge. You can make all the plans you want, worry as much as you want, even try to force your will on people, but at the end of the day, God is in charge.

The "Unseen Hand of God" was on me this whole time, but I felt like it wasn't, and I didn't understand. I knew like Amy, Zack, my Mom and Aiden, I could be spared, and this thing might not be that bad. I knew like my friend Tom; God's will could be different from what I would choose.

All my hopes, dreams and plans were put on hold. Life quickly became day by day, hour by hour, and even at times minute by minute. After a long conversation with my doctor, he strongly advised I leave work and go on short term disability to reduce my stress, spend quality time with my family, and seek appropriate treatment for this, which was not available in the Utica area.

Even for a passionate believer in God, there is no way a moment like this doesn't reset you. There is no way you come out the same on the other side of it. It's natural for some doubts and worries to creep in because we are human. It's living by faith that helps you through it. This is much easier said than done. Trust me, just because people walk through the fire and come out like they are bulletproof, or like it didn't impact them, think again. We are all human. We all struggle. We all doubt. Especially with loved ones we fear leaving behind, or otherwise not be able to take care of them, you fear for them. You want so badly for them not to suffer, even if you have to.

The testimony is to face the mountain, the giant. Face the wide-open ocean. And you have no idea what to do or where to go because you can't see it. That's the point of faith in Hebrews 11:1. Faith is the *evidence* of things *unseen*.

Chapter 26
40 Days and 40 Nights, Part 2

My last day of work was Friday Aug. 11. Two weeks after the first news of a brain tumor, I had just hours to wind down work and pass off all my remaining work and pending business to my teammates. I had many follow-up calls after sending my MRI and medical records to Johns Hopkins, University of Pittsburgh Medical Center, and the University of Rochester. I had to fax and send all kinds of paperwork in to go on disability and run paperwork between doctors and offices. Somehow, during all of this, totally by the grace of God, I closed three deals for work that last day. I felt like I was sprinting to the finish line. I was. I finished at 5 p.m., with no idea how long I'd be out of work and no idea how long treatment would be.

Following the last day of work were hours of late nights up researching my condition and treatment options, and a lot of prayer through many restless nights.

We had a family reunion previously scheduled for Sunday Aug. 13th and it could not have come at a better time. I was surrounded by so much love and prayers from my aunts, uncles and cousins. Change of scenery always helps too.

I had several conversations with friends and family. It was interesting to see the reactions. I quickly realized some people I valued didn't value me as much. Some didn't seem fazed or care about what I was going through. I was surprised whose worlds nearly stopped like mine upon hearing the news and talking to me. Some started crying and would have reached through the phone to hug me if they could.

Those days in the middle of August 2017 turned into a time of taking stock of my life. I truly realized what was most important. And I knew my faith would be tested and deepened.

Within a week, it became clear that God opened the doors to the University of Rochester for treatment and all the other doors were closed. My appointment was Aug. 30th. We had a period to take a breath, think about things, and pray.

As much as you try to keep priorities straight, it's so easy to get sidetracked by things you shouldn't be spending time on or worrying about. You realize some of your goals and dreams were more selfish than anything else. Sometimes we just need a reset. Times like these can turn out to be a huge blessing. Indeed, this was the case for me.

We had planned to homeschool all four kids, but because of my condition, we made the decision to enroll Ariella in our local elementary school, and the twins into a Head Start program. They started getting help that we weren't even aware they needed. A critical blessing that continues to this day with a whole new group of teachers, administrators, counselors and therapists that are a Godsend to our little children.

Amy and I took some much-needed time away together as husband and wife. Mark Enjem and I spent serious time praying and re-evaluating our lives as husbands, fathers and business leaders. I spent the day with my good friend Darrin Harr to get some "mountain therapy" and a lighthearted view of things. His humor is good medicine for anyone. My immediate family surrounded me with encouragement, love and prayer. Our church family were so good to us with unexpected visits, meals, help for the kids and home, prayer, love and encouragement.

Aug. 30th came, and to Rochester we went. After spending most of the day with their team, I got news I wasn't expecting. I was thinking about surgery or at the very least radiation therapy. I was shocked this tumor could be attacked easily by a powerful little pill, Dostinex, which in generic form is called Cabergoline. They said get on it next week, you should be good to go back to work soon and we'll see you in two months for blood work and follow up.

I got on the medicine and it started making a difference almost right away. My energy started to come back, the lethargy started to disappear, and I was lasting longer each day without feeling like I needed a nap. After being on the medicine for two weeks with no major side effects and a double check from my doctor, the clearance was given on Sept. 20th to return to work the next day. And so, ended the second version of 40 days and 40 nights where I was out of work.

Chapter 27
Mamwah

It all started at 4:30 p.m. on Tuesday, March 13, 2018 with a question from my boss. Would our family like tickets to Sesame Street Live? I called my wife to ask her about the tickets for the show. I reminded her that I had a snowmobile ride set up with friends' the night of the show which was two nights later. She said she would call Bonnie and ask if she wanted to go as well. She tried to call Bonnie on both of her cell lines and could not get a hold of her, which was unusual. Since Mamwah lived next-door, Amy called her.

When she did that's when things changed. Mamwah was breathing so hard she could barely talk. It scared the daylights out of Amy, and she knew something had to be done immediately. Not being in a position to run up to the house right away, she called her sister, Jenny, who could get there faster. Amy told Jenny what was going on and alerted her to get to moms soon as possible to bring her to the ER. Jenny got there within 15 minutes, and Bonnie caught up with the messages. They rushed to the hospital.

We then rushed to get Zachary home and to enlist others from the church to help us, since we knew there was a long night ahead of us. By the time Amy and I got there, the next set of news came in which told me that this was it. Septic shock. They drew a lot of blood work and I saw the blood. It did not look like blood. It was like juice, and it was transparent. I alerted Amy's sister Chrissy, who was in Florida on a missions trip, and told her she needed to get on the next flight home.

Overnight and into the early morning of Wednesday, March 14 was both incredibly painful - and inspiring.

Our good friends, the Wengert's, literally dropped everything and stayed up all night for us, fetching anything we needed, and making sure the kids got off to school the next morning. Several people from church came down in the middle of the night to pray with us and comfort us, not caring that they were missing out on sleep. We had no less than 16 people with us as Mamwah entered her final hours in the middle of the night.

Amy and Bonnie were constantly by her side throughout the night, saying "I love you," holding her hand, and praying constantly for God to save her. Bonnie left the room, then shortly after 4 a.m. Mamwah turned to Amy.

She said, "Oh, you're still here".

"Yes, we're leaving for just a little bit. We'll be right back," Amy reassured.

Mamwah said, *"Okay."*

Those were her last words.

Minutes later, she coded.

Though she was brought back, it was only for a few hours. The entire family, our pastor and his family, and many other close family friends gathered to say last goodbyes. We all gathered around holding hands, singing and praying for several minutes. At 9:13 a.m. Wednesday, March 14, 2018, my wife's mother, the most faithful person to God, her family and her church that I had ever met, went to be in the arms of Jesus.

It's easy to praise God when things are good, but in times like these when someone you love so dearly and who loves God so dearly slips away from you on this earth, it can be the ultimate test of your faith. Honestly, for a few weeks after that moment that Mamwah went home to be with the Lord, life stopped. For her four daughters, including Amy, life stopped for much longer. Our dreams were on hold and it was time to grieve. Finding a way forward after such a painful loss is no easier for the faithful Christian than anyone else. We are all human. We are all sinful and fall short of the glory of God. We all struggle.

In the days after her passing, we heard so many testimonies about what Mamwah did in people's lives. We heard how much she cared for strangers, and how faithful she was in prayer for them. Despite my own differences with my mother-in-law, I never appreciated how much she prayed for me. I never appreciated how much she loved me even though we didn't see eye to eye all the time. As a family, we had no idea how many lives she touched outside of church and our own circles. She never talked about it, she never bragged about it, she just did it. It was amazing to see people that we didn't know so choked up about her passing like we were. It was like they had lost their own mother. That is an incredible legacy to leave behind.

Her celebration service 10 days later was amazing. As hard as it was, it was two hours of deep and heartfelt praise to God for such a wonderful woman who raised four kids after losing her husband tragically in the 1970s. She stayed faithful to God no matter how bad things got and had incredible passion to help the people around her. She didn't just say she was praying for them, like a lot of other Christians do, she did pray for them. And she poured her heart and soul into it. Mamwah was there for every church event, every family birthday or special event, and always had her priorities straight. That's a legacy that I want to leave behind for my family. A legacy that we gave everything.

Chapter 28
Weak and weary

No matter who we are, weak or strong, young or old, we all go through those seasons. Professional sports players go through slumps. Some days we don't want to get out of bed. Sometimes the pain of life on this side of heaven is just too much to bear. The mistakes we've made overwhelm us. Or we just want a break because we are so overwhelmed. Raising a teenager is hard. Raising adopted children is harder. Then factor the trauma Ariella had before us, and the twins' special needs.

Add all of this together, including Amy recovering from two major surgeries, 14 weeks apart, which effectively wiped her out for most of 2017, and you have chaos.

That's what was going on in our lives just before Amy had lost her mom. Her hero. The woman who made her the woman you love. She took the sudden loss very hard. Depression set in. She was broken, was having trouble accepting God taking her mom home, trouble going forward because of all the pain.

Writing that, which was our life during the rest of 2018 and going into 2019, makes me amazed as I look at this chapter in the rear-view mirror. I can't believe what we walked through. We strained relationships. Both Amy and I ended up pushing a lot of people away with how we were attempting to handle things. We would overreact, or not react at all. And it was hard for both of us to break away from the self-focused worry and "woe is me" trap you can fall into when life is rough.

There was judgment on Amy for "not getting over" her mom's passing fast enough. If there is one thing, I've learned intimately from seeing what Amy went through and the grief counseling we got, you absolutely don't say that. Your relationship with that person, if you had one, is not the same as others have. Therefore, you will grieve on a different timetable. There is no set timetable on when you should be feeling a certain way. Saying there is or there should be forces your will on someone else. While you think you are doing God's work trying to help them through the pain, you are adding to their pain. The pain of the judgements Amy received, and relationships lost still haunt her to this day. The above is directly referring to "getting over a loss", not using the pain of the loss as an excuse for walking away from God.

There was judgment on me as the extreme stress and pressure of work, taking care of all the kids, being there for Amy in her season of grief, pushed me at times to lose composure. There were a lot of hurtful things I said and did, some of it, without realizing the depth of that hurt. I'll say this much: I never want to be in church again with over 200 people, most of whom you know well, celebrating the end of a great summer Vacation Bible School, followed by a one- hour "come to Jesus" session with several of those same people because of the hurtful things you said and did. Some of this judgement was necessary, especially for this situation. I took responsibility and asked forgiveness.

So, why write this? Why share this? Because it's life. We must stop this stereotype that Christians don't struggle. Being a Christian doesn't mean the absence of struggles. If anything, it means you will have more! Look at what Paul and all the disciples of Jesus went through.

We all go through those seasons. No one is immune. We will never arrive or "get there" on this side of heaven. God is faithful to his children and he does not move. He gives us the free will to move away from him but is right there waiting for you when you are ready to come back to him.

If we are willing to learn and reach towards God, we see that these things which happen to us either by design, the consequences of our own actions, or both, are meant to teach us. Pruning, molding, shaping and making are both destructive and constructive. The destructive part is the changing of what was. The constructive part is allowing the Holy Spirit to move in your life to convict you of your sins and shortcomings and inspire you to change. At the end of it you are better, stronger, wiser, and ready to help others as they go through their seasons.

We must learn and accept that the days of fear, doubt, helplessness, hopelessness and worthlessness will come. The fact that these days and times comes to us doesn't reveal the strength of our relationship, how "together" we have things or how "spiritual" we are. It's when we enter those seasons, and come back to Jesus, the realization we are nothing without him (John 15:5), the fact that we need his power to go forward (Philippians 4:13) and the fact that most of the time we don't have the answers as to why. It's a walk of faith (Hebrews 11:1).

It's how we work through these seasons, through the grief, through the pain of things we didn't ask to happen to us, through the consequences of our own sinful, selfish and poor decisions. That process of realizing who we are, and more importantly who we are **in Christ** that we learn what we need to learn, draw closer to God, draw closer to each other, grow in faith and in maturity. It's messy. Life is messy. And that's OK.

I don't know where would be without people like our friends Jim & Carol, my good friends Darrin Harr and Mark Enjem, and our family. It's the love, grace, and forgiveness they gave to Amy and especially to me that helped get us through. We are not meant to be alone in our struggles. We are meant to be in relationships not just with the Lord Jesus but with each other.

It's not something that happens overnight but is a process. The important thing is this: Are you doing the right things?

While this was going on, I pushed ahead by trying to advance into management at work.

I thought I had a good shot. But I was passed up. The way I found out was hard and it took me a little time to get over the anger, selfishness thinking you were the man for the job, and being weary from constantly striving for advancement only to come up short. I didn't understand why I had the desire to lead through the struggles with my own family, and constantly coming up short in my career work. It didn't make any sense at the time. In waiting on the answers from God on everything personal and professional, it drove me to the exact place that God wanted me to be.

Chapter 29
Acceptance

The acceptance of God's will. This is the place where God wants us. Thy will, not my will. I am a clear example of someone who thinks he has it figured out, wants to know everything, leave no stone unturned, know the why and know what to do.

It just doesn't work like that. How can I truly have faith and trust in the God of this universe, the King of Kings, Lord of Lords, the one whom created me, sent his only son Jesus to die for me, yet I continually fall into the lie and trap that somehow he doesn't understand nor have the power to help me through my situations?

After failing to advance in career, failing to keep my wife from falling into a deep depression after the sudden passing of her mom, and watching Zachary get crushed by the struggles of being a teenager in this world, to the point our happy and hilarious son was broken and hopeless though a confessing believer in Christ; watching our adopted little ones hurt because they didn't have the time, attention, and love they needed and so desperately wanted... it brought me to this:

We needed to accept.

Accept the fact that we are here in this place and in these circumstances and we have no idea what to do next. We literally had to cry out to God that we don't know what to do.

Heading into the spring of 2019, that's where I was. So was Amy.

We had to accept that our lives were truly not our own. As much as we think we have control, we don't. He does. Yes, he gives us the freedom to do what we want. We think we have control and can strive for whatever we want. And after we get over ourselves, come back to God. Make things right. Ask him for the power and strength to do the things that only He can do through us, when we are obedient and submissive to his will. His will for our lives, our families, our careers, and our ministry to others.

It's not complicated. It's simple. Like salvation being a gift to receive and not something to earn, it takes something so hard to do, yet so simple and easy.

Accept. Accept the fact you can't get to heaven without Jesus Christ dying on the cross for you. Accept the fact you can't do anything good without his power and strength. Accept the fact there is no other way. Accept the fact he may bring you down roads you wouldn't go down willingly. Accept the fact he will answer your prayers in his will, his timing and his terms. That's because he loves you. It's like you as a father or mother to your child, God wants the best for us.

We must come to that place before he can work in us. If I wasn't ready to accept what he had for me next, how would that work out?

It was at that point I accepted; I may never advance beyond where I was in my career. I accepted I couldn't be the husband I needed to be to Amy, the father I needed to be to my children, the man I needed to be with all those around me, it was only at that point that God can finally do the work in me he needed to do. Once I reached the point of faith, obedience to his will, whatever it was and **acceptance** for whatever he had for me next, is when HIS will, not mine, and the healing would come.

Chapter 30
Floodgates

Over the next few months, into the summer of 2019, some amazing opportunities started to happen. People started reaching out to me for management career opportunities. Some of it was very tempting and lucrative but would have required uprooting my family. After much prayer and consideration, especially after what we had just been through, it was not the right time. Turning down big money is hard, and most people won't do it. They'll take the money. And, trust me, when you have a mortgage, car payments, loan payments and four children to raise, you need money to survive. I get it. And I'm totally there with the bills to pay.

The biblical order of things is clear. God first, then spouse (if you have one), then children (if you have them), then your family, then your work, then everything else. If you go too far down the list to fill that and make that most important, you will throw everything else out of balance into chaos. I was determined not to do that. I know how much God loves me, my wife loves me, and my children love me. I had to rest in faith that the right opportunity, the right situation in the right place, would be revealed. God would provide the needs, even if it wasn't the money that others would offer or that you feel you would deserve.

The professional opportunity came, and in a way that only God could orchestrate. While I was evaluating and ready to pursue other opportunities I thought God was bringing me to, it was a lunch conversation and what happened in the weeks to follow that set me on the path to where I had wanted to be.

Wayne Taylor had lunch with me in late June 2019 and said something I wasn't expecting: "Would you be interested in working for us part or full time again?" I had worked with Wayne, General Manager, of the Mars Hill Network, a Christian media organization based in Syracuse, NY, in the early 2010's when I had my own company, working as their on-air meteorologist and one of their personalities on weekends.

Our working relationship was forced to end at the end of 2014 when a previous employer had called "conflict of interest." I had permission originally from that employer to do outside weather focused work through my own company on my own time for 10 months but they revoked it in a late-night phone call out of the blue and gave me 30 days to end my weather business or lose my job with them. I not only had to give up working for the Mars Hill Network at the time, but upstatesnow.com, which is a popular winter weather and snowmobile enthusiast website I launched in 2012. I also had to give up other private weather contracts which never would have any implications in the work I was in at that time. This was all despite exceeding goals and expectations for the employer and being one of their top performers.

Wayne understood at the time, and we stayed in touch. He felt bad for what happened and always said if the opportunity came, we would hope to work together again. There was nothing available at that time, and what would have been a perfect job for me, director of development, was just filled and the candidate was ready to start in a few weeks. I figured that door to working for them was closed as this position was filled and no others were available at that time. Though we wanted to do something together, it wasn't meant to be, or so I thought.

I had faith as the floodgates were thrown open on career opportunities, healing was coming for Amy, our marriage, and healing for and with our children, it was but a matter of time. I came across a note I had sent to our inner circle, dated July 10, 2019. It seemed insignificant at the time but looking back it was chilling and almost prophetic. I will share some of it:

Good evening! I hope your summer is going well so far.

As you may remember from around this time last year, I was finishing up and about to publish my first book, Unseen Hand of God... Then all the sudden, nothing. What happened? I had everything completed including the audiobook and everything ready to publish on Amazon in October of 2018. I had all approvals... At the last moment, literally days before publishing, I was told to hold on... and never got the go to proceed again.

There is a reason for everything. It's God's story, not mine, I'm just a character in his story. It's ultimately a testimony to him and about him about what he has done through me, despite me. I never doubted for a moment it will be published and see the light of day, someday, but God's timing is perfect. I rest in it. I trust in it. I never forced the writing or timelines at all on this journey, the three-year anniversary of which is this upcoming Monday July 15th, after hearing Dr. Woodrow Kroll at Word of Life.

So, what now? As I have prayed, sought input from my wife, my family and trusted mentors, I have been led to make modifications to the book. The title will be slightly different: Unseen Hand of God, A Journey of Faith, Family and Second Chances. The focus will be solely on my faith and how God miraculously brought my family to be what it is today. Some chapters will be taken out, new ones added. The timeline for this process is unknown. A publish date is still unknown. Only God knows at this point.

It has become clear to me is that in the short term I have a great job with providence and stability for my wife and kids. If forcing to publish the book will jeopardize this, I will not...

Notwithstanding I have had a growing desire to write (many more books than this one), speak (not just to churches but to organizations, public or anyone willing to entertain and enthusiastic and positive message on a range of topics) and more fully through all my work use the gift of communication that God has given me. To encourage, entertain, educate, inspire, and ultimately fulfill my personal (and I believe God given) mission: Help people every day, in every way, regardless of what it is.

In the long term, I believe God will work out the transition to where he ultimately wants me in terms of work, the publishing of this book, any future ones, and where he leads me and my family next. Until such a time, I have been convicted I need to work diligently towards this end. Hence why my writing will restart after a 9-month hiatus. My wife and I will seek other work and ways to make and save money, to make a transition from where I work now less of a financial burden to bear.

I ask you to pray for me and my family on this journey. Finally, when the time comes, I ask for your feedback and prayers on future projects and opportunities as God brings them about. I cannot thank you enough for your prayers, encouragement and love to me and my family. God bless you. Until we talk again soon, Rich"

A few days later, my phone buzzed. I was walking into Pastor Cecil's office for a meeting when Wayne emailed me. The candidate hired for director of development backed out. The position was open again. He wanted me to interview for it. I had said in that moment to Cecil, it looks like I'm going to be working for Mars Hill Network. I just knew the moment I saw the email that it was the answer. I went through the process, I interviewed, and Wayne chose to hire me. The dream for leadership had come true. The opportunity to grow as a leader had come. The opportunity for full-time ministry, a growing desire and dream of mine in recent years, to live out the things most important to me, my faith and family, had come. But this is not where it ends. The floodgates were still open.

I let go of my project, upstatesnow.com, five years earlier when I was forced to end my outside company. The good friend who bought it from me and took it over, and the meteorologist I gave the weather forecasting opportunities to, had also hit a crossroad. Dave was not able to keep it going, and Chris, who did the weather, had just accepted an offer to be a teacher, with a track to get his masters and teaching certification. Both of their lives were diverging away from upstatesnow.com at the first opportunity I had in five years to be able to take it back. Dave and I made the deal. Zack, who is much older, and experienced in both snowmobiling and video production now, besides being a bigger snow freak than me, encouraged me to take it back.

It would be a challenge with the extra work for us, but there is a purpose and love for it shared by me and my oldest son. We are doing the project as father and son. Snowmobiling has become for me and Zack our father son thing, our bonding time, our special times together that will last a lifetime. That's the driving force behind this. We are sharing our love for winter and snowmobiling from this angle, everything that is good and positive about the sport, and the testimony of our relationship with each other and the Lord to tens of thousands of people who are Facebook fans and that view the site monthly in the winter months here.

Like Mars Hill Network, this was not something I asked for. It was brought to me by God. I had set both free, though I loved them, five years ago. And God brought them both back to me. In his will and timing, on his terms. The people who have come into my life in the second half of 2019, the opportunities that have come into my life during this same time, have been incredible. Add to this the greatest Christmas present one could ever receive. In December after my annual MRI I was told the brain tumor was "biologically inert". In other words, DEAD. The matter is still in there but is no longer jeopardizing my health or my life at this time. Heading into 2020, a new year, a new decade, the floodgates remain wide open with incredible challenges, but also incredible blessings and opportunities.

Through our struggles and shortcomings, my marriage with Amy has grown stronger. After my salvation through Jesus Christ, she is the best thing that has ever happened to me. The unconditional and undeserved love we have for each other, is powered by the undeserved love we have from Jesus Christ. The love and forgiveness we have had to give each other has been immense. That has caused our love for each other to grow deeper, and the love for our family. It is truly special, a miracle, what we have. I'm so thankful we see it, know it is a loving God and his son Jesus that has made all of this and everything to come, possible.

When we work in the power of the Holy Spirit, through God the Father and Jesus Christ the son, the floodgates open.

Chapter 31
Looking to the future

I still have so far to go, so much to learn, and there's no credit I can take for this life. It's the evidence of a living God that loves me and cares for me. It's all about what God has done through me, **despite me**.

Let me repeat that again. It's not me. **It's despite me**.

We all get selfish; we are all human, we all have bad days and make mistakes. No matter how good or "spiritual" you are, or how high of a position of leadership or influence you have in business or in ministry, **no one is immune.** I have personally seen it. Pride goes before the fall, Proverbs 16:18. If you have people in your life that seem immune to being human, making mistakes and falling short, may I suggest you look for others to lead you. Having real people that are humble and real is what we need. I purpose myself to be real and not fake. If I make a mistake, I will own up to it, learn from it and grow from it.

The world condemns you. God corrects you. Fake Christians and fake friends will gossip about you, backstab, hurt you and will tear you down while feeling a sense of pride that they are doing God's work. Real Christians and real friends stick by you through the trial, help you, be patient with you, and celebrate with you as you come through on the other side. I've met both. I know what I want to be and what I want around me, my family and friends.

If you want to change your life, get with people who are real. They are out there. Leave the fakers behind to indulge in their self-righteousness. They've already hurt enough people in this world.

People say it, and it's true. Don't give in to the fear. Back in the 90's, "No Fear" T-shirts were popular. They were popular because the philosophy is true. Here is what I've learned personally:

Fear takes from you what God wants to give you.

You will regret the opportunities you don't take.

You may get another chance. You may not. I can guarantee you if it's a good woman (or man), you are highly unlikely to get another chance at something as good as now.

Don't live to work, Work to live!

LOVE is spelled TIME

**God put you here for a reason.
Don't second guess him.**

God gave you a job. See it through.

God gave you a family. Love them. Don't give up on them. You wouldn't want them to give up on you.

If God takes away peace in doing something (or meeting someone), go with your gut. Your gut a lot of times is the Holy Spirit's way to reaching you since we're too busy talking or thinking of what to say next. Be careful as the heart can deceive you, always go to God in prayer before taking action.

Finally, it's counter intuitive, but you must do it like this: **Focus on what you are giving, rather than what you are receiving.**

I want to give my wife, my children, my family and friends so much. Not in things, but love, friendship, attention, confidence, and trust. I want to spend my life being a servant leader, following Jesus Christ, the son of God, my redeemer.

So, where do I go from here? Wherever God takes me. It may be full of fun. It may be full of pain. I'll learn a lot along the way. I believe all those things will be true of me regardless of what happens. The challenges are there and even more so with a profession of faith like this. I don't want to do it, but I love my God and want to be faithful to him.

What do I want to do from here? **Work hard. Play hard. Love recklessly. Live humbly and thankfully.** I want to share this story with as many people as possible.

Whatever you do, don't put the focus on me, anything I say, or put me up on a pedestal. I don't deserve it; I don't belong there. I'm just being faithful to the calling God has given me and I fully believe he has given me the talent and experiences to do it well. I want to turn this around to help you, encourage you, inspire you, and challenge you. I want to see people fully place their faith and trust in God and in his son Jesus Christ. It's God who gets the glory because it's a story about him, his faithfulness and love for me. His story, not mine.

Regardless of what happens, big or small, or wherever God takes me, my number one priority is to worship and serve him. That's not only wise, it's biblical. The next priority is my wife Amy. I need to be the husband she needs. I need to honor, love, cherish and respect her always. Following Amy are Zachary, Ariella, Lillian and Aiden. Our world changed for the better because God brought them into our lives. They are the greatest gifts we'll ever have on this Earth. I need to be the father that is not just present but engaged, pouring my life into them, teaching them, leading them and guiding them until they are ready to spread their wings and fly on their own. Love is spelled T-I-M-E. The extended family and friends follow that.

Finally, there is our work and our ministry. I'm incredibly blessed to be able to work full time in ministry, sharing my faith and my family, serving others, sharing our love for essential oils with others (We love Young Living's essential oils), and going where God needs us. Until such time, we will be faithful to the fields God has placed us in now. We will be content wherever he has us.

It's a hard balance. The demands of life eat at you from all sides and if you care like I do, you don't want to let people down. But there needs to be balance. This goes not just for me, but for all of us. *As for me and my house, we will serve the Lord* (Joshua 24:15 ESV). And regardless of how easy or hard it is from this day forward; I need to follow Matthew 5:14-16.

Share my story and give God the glory.

Chapter 32
Second Chances

    Like life, you're not perfect. You're going to mess it up. It's not about perfection, but the direction. When you stumble and fall, it's how you get up and move on the right way. Don't give into the lie of what you see on social media about everyone's lives. Dare I say that's "fake news!" It's what they want you to see. Stop the façade. Be real. There's enough fake in the world. Don't be a part of it. Be real.

    Another thing you see is judgement, condemnation and the tearing down of people. Social media sometimes becomes a virtual Roman Coliseum. When somebody says something they shouldn't, makes a verbal mistake, or shares a worldview that is not what a certain group wants or demands, we must destroy them! We must show them! "How dare you? How could you? I would never do that! I would never say that! You are _____."

    I've personally watched as people's lives have been destroyed by mistakes. Even if the mistakes were bad, the mob mentality and desire to pile on, insult, judge, ridicule is downright scary. The worst part about this? Some truly good-hearted people I know participate in this, wittingly or unwittingly.

    How many times have you seen it? How many times have you participated in it? Answer honestly. Regardless of your answer, get up and go look in the mirror. No, really, literally, get up and go look at yourself in the mirror. Look at yourself. Do you like what you see? Now stick your tongue out, like a little kid, then look at that tongue for a minute. That little thing can control the rest of you and have a bearing on others. Do you really want it to be for good? I challenge you to read all of James chapter 3, especially the first 12 verses. If you don't like it or believe in the Bible, fair enough, go back to what I said in the very first chapter about treating others the way you want to be treated, so we are all on the same page here.

Your words have great power. They can build up or they can tear down. Regardless of what you have been, you have the power to change things going forward. What do you want it to be? What do you want others to see when they see you? Do you want them to see someone easily offended, vengeful and unforgiving? Do you think that is attractive to them? Do you want them to see someone willing to listen, be calm, respectful and measured in their response? Someone who would want to give them another chance to do better? Right the wrong?

As you have seen from my testimony, my life story, it is riddled with mistakes. It's also riddled with second chances. Go back to a point in the story and change in your mind for a moment what happened. Change what happened to condemning me. Ridiculing me. Firing me. Doing whatever to me, for what I did or said earlier in my life. Scorch the earth. I don't deserve it, I'm a terrible human being that doesn't deserve to live because I did one thing or said something intentional or not.

Then what? Now what? Would you have the story you are reading right now? **No.** Would I still be married? **No.** Would everyone be better off? **No.**

Would you be better off???
NO.

Part of the problem we have in this culture, part of the problem we have in our churches, and in our lives is the fact that second chances are now few and far between, or in some cases non-existent. No wonder why suicide rates are skyrocketing! No wonder why so many people are depressed! No wonder why so many people have lost hope! If God didn't give us a second chance by sending his son Jesus Christ, we'd all be doomed!

How can you expect those around you to love you, get better, and heal, if you don't provide them the opportunity? How can you expect people that have made public mistakes, intentional or unintentional, to get better, learn from it and grow? If you completely destroy them, you can't. Because there is nothing left. But I've given them so many chances! They keep screwing up. They just don't get it. I've had enough! They'll never learn. They'll never get it. I give up! My pastor recently did a sermon on Luke 13:1-9. Read that, especially verses 6-9, the parable of the barren fig tree. Just because some people take longer or require more effort, does not mean they are any less deserving of grace than you.

What does the Bible say about forgiveness? Go to the Parable of the Unforgiving Servant in Matthew chapter 18, verses 21-35. It's below in the ESV version. Before you read this, here's a thought to ponder. Even after God judged Israel many times in the Old Testament, he still restored them. Earlier in Matthew, the Prodigal son. There was no limit on his wrongs for when he finally saw the light, he went back to his father. His Father forgave him and celebrated coming home. God did the same for Israel. God will do the same for you. Here's the parable:

"Then Peter came up and said to him, "Lord, how often will my brother sin against me, and I forgive him? As many as seven times?" Jesus said to him, "I do not say to you seven times, but seventy-seven times.

"Therefore the kingdom of heaven may be compared to a king who wished to settle accounts with his servants. When he began to settle, one was brought to him who owed him ten thousand talents. And since he could not pay, his master ordered him to be sold, with his wife and children and all that

he had, and payment to be made. So the servant fell on his knees, imploring him, 'Have patience with me, and I will pay you everything.' And out of pity for him, the master of that servant released him and forgave him the debt.

But when that same servant went out, he found one of his fellow servants who owed him a hundred denarii, and seizing him, he began to choke him, saying, 'Pay what you owe.' So, his fellow servant fell down and pleaded with him, 'Have patience with me, and I will pay you.' He refused and went and put him in prison until he should pay the debt. When his fellow servants saw what had taken place, they were greatly distressed, and they went and reported to their master all that had taken place. Then his master summoned him and said to him, 'You wicked servant! I forgave you all that debt because you pleaded with me. And should not you have had mercy on your fellow servant, as I had mercy on you?' And in anger his master delivered him to the jailers, until he should pay all his debt. So also my heavenly Father will do to every one of you, if you do not forgive your brother from your heart."

So, what are you going to do? Do you want your story to be a comeback story? Do you want to be the one to help people out in their time of need? Do you want to be more like Christ? Give people what they need, your best, your love, your patience, forgiveness, and a second chance.

This world would be a whole lot better place if each of us start living like that. Because the whole story of Christ even coming for us was a second chance, after Adam and Eve. The world was perfect in the garden with Adam and Eve until sin entered it, and then the world. Jesus was the second chance. I have been given a second chance by grace through God the Father and Jesus the son. My family, friends and others have given me many second chances. And I've taken them. And we are all blessed because of it.

You have a second chance now. Give it to God. You have a second chance to give second chances to others. They may not accept, and if they don't, Romans 12:18, as far as it depends on you, live at peace with everyone. Do your part. It may not be time. It may not happen. But be faithful to the work.

Give that second chance. Take that second chance. Watch what happens as the "Unseen Hand of God" works through whatever it is you need. Then share the story. And give God the glory. Rinse. Repeat.

Thank you for letting me share this with you. May God use this to bless you, and all those around you. Give God the credit. I am simply his vessel, walking in faith to him.

Until next time,
Rich

About the Author

Rich Lupia was born and raised in Utica, NY. He is a 1993 graduate of Proctor High School (formerly Utica Senior Academy). He received a Bachelor of Science degree in Atmospheric Science from the University at Albany in 1997. He has worked in television, radio, print media, digital and did all the above in his own business at one point! That business, Lupia & Associates LLC, is the company that published this book and also owns and operates www.upstatesnow.com, a snowmobile enthusiast, winter weather forecast and winter recreation website serving upstate New York. Rich currently serves as Director of Development for the Mars Hill Network, a Christian media organization based in Syracuse, N.Y.

He has been married to his wife Amy since 2001 and has four children, Zachary, Ariella, Lillian and Aiden. He loves helping people and encouraging people regardless of their location and position in life.

Rich is happy to speak to groups and organizations, sharing his life experiences, motivating people from all walks of life to persevere and rise above the challenges in front of them. To reach out to Rich you may contact the following:

Appearance Requests: richlupia@protonmail.com
Website: http://www.richlupia.com
Facebook: http://www.facebook.com/unseenhandofgod
Instagram: http://www.instagram.com/rlupia

©2020 Lupia & Associates LLC
All rights reserved

Acknowledgements

First and foremost, to God and his son Jesus Christ – I am nothing without you. From a grateful servant that does not deserve life more abundantly here on this Earth, much less eternity in heaven with you: May this work and what happens next be to your glory and not mine.

To my incredible wife Amy – I love you always and forever. I'm so grateful for your faithful love and encouragement to me and our family through the good and the bad. I don't deserve such an incredible woman as you.

To Zachary – Our only son born to us. You are an incredible young man. We are so proud of you. Your humor and love for life is amazing. May you never lose that humor, your heart for God and your incredible compassion for others.

To Ariella – Your story will change the world. Your compassion for others is amazing. Your artistry is inspiring. Never give up your smile, your love or your curly hair! Keep your fierce heart and spirit!

To Lillian – Your energy and love are incredible. Never lose your fearlessness or your tender heart. You are a great woman in the making. Your desire to work hard and to do the right thing will carry you far.

To Aiden – You are a walking miracle with the heart of a lion. Your smile and your strength despite the incredible pain you've had to endure through your young life have been inspiring to so many. Don't ever let your limitations limit you.

To mom and dad – Thank you for loving me, raising me old school with respect for others, inspiration to reach my dreams and a great work ethic you've given to me. Thank you for never giving up on me. I owe you more than I could ever repay.

To Amy's sisters Bonnie, Jenny and Chrissy – Thank you for your love, grace and patience with me through the years. I wish I had you growing up, but I'm thankful to have you now.

To Kevin DeValk and family – I am grateful for your friendship and for helping me by editing this book. You knew what I needed, and I thank God you are in my life. You have so much to look forward to and I'm so happy for you!

To Mark Enjem – My best friend. My wingman. My sounding board. Thank you for your faithful prayers and encouragement through the ups and downs and for my countless interruptions at Enjem's. You've been there through it all.

To Darrin Harr – God made us for such a time as this. I am so blessed to have you as a close friend, your unique perspective, and the honor to ride with the snowmobiling king. Your passion for riding, serving and family is inspiring.

To Cindy Santos – You have been an angel to our family. Thank you for your faithful prayers for us, being there for us when the chips were down, and being so generous with us. Your southern hospitality and servants' heart are incredible!

To Rance Choate – Dog! I am forever grateful to you for showing me by example what life in Christ is like. Thank you for never giving up on me. The example of Christ you have set in your family is multiplying. Keep on serving brother!

To Pastor Cecil and family –Your stories are so much more powerful than mine and the world needs to hear them. Tell them. Write the books! Keep leading in love.

To Pastor Mark and family – Thank you for the love, grace and teaching you poured into us. We love you! You always have been and always will be like family to us all.

To Jim and Carol – Thank you for being there for Amy while growing up, and for how you've cared for us like family. Your faithful prayers and generosity to our family is amazing.

To Wayne Taylor – You have been a great mentor, leader and friend for many years to me. Thank you for the once in a lifetime chance and for your support of my developing dreams.

To my extended family, aunts, uncles and especially my cousins: You are loved, and you are missed. I wish we can get together more often than we do. I'm grateful for each one of you. May we get together more often like old days.

To my friends: Thank you for being a positive influence on my life. I'm grateful for each one of you. I pray that I'm a blessing to you and if I haven't been lately, that I will be in the future. May we also get together more often than we do.

Finally, to you: My prayer is that you've been blessed by the story and pay it forward by encouraging others, loving one another, and sharing your story to the hurting people around us all. Thank you for investing into my work, now invest into others!!!

A Dios Sea La Gloria…

Rich

Made in the USA
Middletown, DE
05 March 2020